"The beautifully fashioned sentences throughout *Broken Hallelujahs* summon deep contemplation and provoke a wrestling with the realities of our mysterious lives. What is truly refreshing about *Broken Hallelujahs* is the absence of sentimentalism. With a timely cadence, this book moved me to tears—tears of grief, loss and lament, but also tears of joyfulness and gratitude. Beth's willingness to be vulnerable and to call a thing what it is gave me permission to sink into the profound truth that Jesus Christ shows us it is truly human to sometimes cry out, 'My God, why have you forsaken me?' *Broken Hallelujahs* ministered to my soul like a balm of Gilead. I love this book and hope you will take care of your soul by reading this astonishing story."

Mike King, president and CEO, Youthfront, author of *Presence Centered Youth Ministry*

"This book provides a needed resource for anyone struggling to stay connected with God in the midst of faith-shaking turmoil and loss. Beth's courageous vulnerability encourages her readers to equal honesty, while the spiritual practices that close each chapter offer a means of experiencing God without denying the human emotions that accompany loss. It is a book I will read and reread, and one that I will share with others. For who has not experienced the grief and loss that are part of every life?"

Elizabeth L. Patterson, former associate dean, School of Theology, Fuller Theological Seminary

"I don't normally think of grief and beauty cozying up with one another. But that's the indelible impression this gorgeous book imprinted on my heart and mind. Slevcove—with sometimes startling vulnerability and relentless authenticity—opens up her journey into and through grief, shining a light on something far, far better than simple platitudes or greeting card perk pills. This book reveals truth. And it's the best kind of truth, messy and heart-wrenching and full of the potency of new life."

Mark Oestreicher, The Youth Cartel, author of *Hopecasting*

"Beth's personal story joined with her theological reflections becomes a paradigm for those on the path of spiritual maturity. This book is simply eloquent, profoundly wise, inspiring and practical. It is a truly fresh perspective on the reality of grieving our losses as we progress through our lives."

Francis Benedict, OSB, a monk of St. Andrew's Abbey in Valyermo, California

"All of us have experienced loss in some way, but too often we don't take the time to grieve that loss, and most of us, myself included, don't even know *how* to begin to process the loss so we can move toward healing. Beth's new book *Broken Hallelujahs* is a beautiful reflection on loss and love and finding God again after God's silence. Through her stories and the exercises and practices included at the end of each chapter, Beth gives us the tools we need to process our grief and help us connect to God and actually move on toward healing."

Lilly Lewin, author of *Sacred Space* and founder of ThinplaceNashville

"Beth Slevcove chronicles her story of disappointment and grief and invites us to see the hidden beauty of the dark and lonely places in our own lives. With the gentleness of a spiritual director, she offers earthy and practical wisdom for navigating life's inevitable difficulties. This book makes me hungry to discover paths through pain and loss that are more honest, creative and God-conscious."

Mark Scandrette, author of *Free* and *Practicing the Way of Jesus*

"Loss and grief, if confronted alone, can leave us feeling abandoned and despairing. But when given the perspective of a wise, experienced—and above all—tender guide, it can lead to wellspring of a deeper life. Writing in prose that bends toward poetry, Beth Slevcove is precisely such a guide. Using her own losses and her own life to lead us to the truths that lie amidst our own life fragments, Beth asks and attends to the hardest questions of life and faith with candor, courage, vulnerability and a wit that will make you sigh deeply and smile amidst your tears. This is a simply splendid book."

Tod Bolsinger, vice president for vocation and formation, Fuller Theological Seminary, author of *Canoeing the Mountains*

"In *Broken Hallelujahs* Beth Allen Slevcove gives us a beautifully written, deeply personal account of her experience of loss—its pain and its potential. As I read it, I began to see some of my own experience of loss through the lens she provided. Reading her story is a hopeful encounter, one I would wish for anyone struggling with loss. And at some point, that will be all of us."

John Hambrick, Buckhead Church, Atlanta, author of *Move Toward the Mess*

"My Sunday School faith prepared me to approach life with an expectation of happily ever after. But at some point it became clear that life really is broken. If we are not prepared for this—and few of us are—it can lead to disillusionment and loss of faith. In this beautiful book, Beth Slevcove invites us to accompany her on her own journey of loss and tragedy. I often cried along as I recognized many elements in common with my own experience. I was challenged by her determination to find God in the midst of it without turning away from reality. In the end, her ability to still say hallelujah through the tears and in the midst of the mess is deeply inspiring. This is a charming, sometimes poetic book with profound insights, and it is also a book that I will return to again and again, since each chapter ends with prayer practices and exercises for seeking and occasionally wrestling with God."

Scott Sabin, executive director, Plant With Purpose

"Not just another good grief book but a helpful journey through grief from happy hallelujahs to broken hallelujahs, and in the midst of multiple losses, finally to the hopeful hallelujah of faith and endurance."

Michael J. Christensen, Wesley Center, Point Loma Nazarene University

"Beth Slevcove has provided us with the quintessential primer on learning how to 'grieve the big and small losses of life.' No one would ask for any of these losses to come their way. Yet, in all the losses that Beth has experienced, she has and continues to be attentive to holding all before God, offering her own deep response to the pain again, and again, and again. Throughout the book we are provided with the privilege and opportunity to do the same. And you know what? Over time, we may discover that the broken hallelujahs in our own lives are the very things that take us deeper into the unbroken hallelujah. O may it be so! Thank you, Beth."

Maggie Robbins, spiritual director, coauthor of *Enjoy the Silence*

"Beth is a singularly unique person. When you meet her, it's clear there is no box to put her in—she's equal parts theologian, mystic, surfer chick and earth mother. In *Broken Hallelujahs*, Beth invites us along as she explores her personal losses and her learnings about God in the process, offering spiritual practices that can help us do the same."

Elaine Martens Hamilton, marriage and family therapist, founder and director, The Soul Care House

BROKEN
HALLELUJAHS

LEARNING TO GRIEVE THE BIG
AND SMALL LOSSES OF LIFE

Beth Allen Slevcove

≋
IVP Books
An imprint of InterVarsity Press
Downers Grove, Illinois

InterVarsity Press
P.O. Box 1400, Downers Grove, IL 60515-1426
ivpress.com
email@ivpress.com

InterVarsity Press® is the book-publishing division of InterVarsity Christian Fellowship/USA®, a movement of students and faculty active on campus at hundreds of universities, colleges and schools of nursing in the United States of America, and a member movement of the International Fellowship of Evangelical Students. For information about local and regional activities, visit intervarsity.org.

Scripture quotations, unless otherwise noted, are from the New Revised Standard Version of the Bible, copyright 1989 by the Division of Christian Education of the National Council of the Churches of Christ in the USA. Used by permission. All rights reserved.

While any stories in this book are true, some names and identifying information may have been changed to protect the privacy of individuals.

Excerpt from the poem "First Lessons" by Philip Booth, in Lifelines: Selected Poems 1950–1999 *(New York: Penguin, 1999), is used by permission.*

Some excerpts were previously published as "Losing My Religion," Immerse Journal, *March/April 2012, and "Broken Hallelujahs: Rediscovering the Art of Grieving in a Culture That Doesn't,"* Immerse Journal, *September/October 2012.*

Cover design: Cindy Kiple
Interior design: Beth McGill
Images: broken flower: © Stolk/iStockphoto
photo on dedication page by Laura Allen; headshot of author by Laura Allen

ISBN 978-0-8308-4323-7 (print)
ISBN 978-0-8308-9922-7 (digital)

Printed in the United States of America ∞

Library of Congress Cataloging-in-Publication Data
Names: Slevcove, Beth Allen, 1968- author.
Title: Broken hallelujahs : learning to grieve the big and small losses of life / Beth Allen Slevcove.
Description: Downers Grove : InterVarsity Press, 2016. | Includes bibliographical references.
Identifiers: LCCN 2015050913 (print) | LCCN 2016001643 (ebook) | ISBN 9780830843237 (pbk. : alk. paper) | ISBN 9780830899227 (eBook)
Subjects: LCSH: Suffering—Religious aspects—Christianity. | Loss (Psychology)—Religious aspects—Christianity. | Grief—Religious aspects—Christianity.
Classification: LCC BV4909 .S565 2016 (print) | LCC BV4909 (ebook) | DDC 248.8/6—dc23
LC record available at http://lccn.loc.gov/2015050913

P	20	19	18	17	16	15	14	13	12	11	10	9	8	7	6	5	4	3	2	1
Y	32	31	30	29	28	27	26	25	24	23	22	21	20	19	18	17	16			

for Mark,

the true author of the family

Contents

Part 2: Listening to Our Losses

Part 3: Inviting Hope

Introduction

Hallelujah, INITIALLY UNDERSTOOD in my forming lexicon to mean "Hooray!" was sung with gusto often accompanied by guitar and clapping. Ha-la-la-la-la-la-la-le-lu-jah came wafting out the bus windows as we wound our way up the mountain to summer camp, stretching the potent Hebrew holy word around our happy bursts of prepubescent excitement.

As life began gathering more sharps and flats and my internal melody shifted from the brighter, cheerier major chords to some darker minors, "Hooray!" was not always an accurate descriptor. I left the word *hallelujah* and the shallow theologies it seemed to embody on the shelf next to the stuffed animals and Sunday school loot acquired in memory verse contests. I was beginning to believe that this word, and to some degree its holy recipient, no longer spoke to the situations at hand.

"Just give it to God" was not working, so I tried to toughen up and pretend hurtful things did not hurt me, to "just get over" the painful parts of life. This, too, did not work.

I eventually figured out that grief was the way through.

Grieving allows us to live beyond the narrow sliver of existence, numb to both the lows of loss and the delight-filled gifts of grace.

I am beginning to recognize that my journeys of loss are not interruptions to life but essential vehicles to engage in life more deeply. As the adage reminds us, "What is in the way *is* the way." Instead of thinking, "If I can only get around this hurdle, I'll be able to really start living," I'm learning to say yes to God in all that life brings. In doing so, I am not condoning the bad things that happen but acknowledging that God is there too, in the midst of all of life, actively leading me home.

One of my favorite songs is Leonard Cohen's perplexing and beautiful "Hallelujah." In it, he gorgeously weaves raw stories of fallen human beings who cry out "Hallelujah" from the midst of brokenness. He calls it "a cold" and "broken Hallelujah." Thanks to this song and an assortment of undesirable life experiences, *hallelujah* has become one of the most powerful words I know, a word capable of unapologetically lashing great pain and disillusionment to heartfelt praise, a seemingly impossible task. Yet this is our task. Living into the contradictory realities of brokenness and beauty *is* the spiritual journey. It's not an easy journey, but it's the only one that allows us to fully engage in the sacred symphony of life.

I begin the book by telling *my stories* of loss in hopes that you will find some of your own stories begin to open. The second part broadens into *our stories*, incorporating what I've noticed and learned both personally and as a spiritual director. The third part moves into ways I have engaged creatively in loss in order to make room for hope, inviting you to do the same.

At the end of every chapter, I introduce various classic and creative prayer practices that have helped me in my journeys through loss. These practices encourage honest conversation with God, allowing our reflections to drop down into the presence of the One who holds and heals. If they feel forced or contrived to you (as exercises in books often do to me) then skip over them; if they feel inviting and helpful, jump in.

I invite you to use my thoughts and stories to enter deeply into your own journey of broken hallelujahs with a renewed sense of hope. *L'chaim!* To life!

part one

WHAT'S BEEN LOST?

- one -

Remembering Eden

We have to leave the garden.
It is only important that you have
a garden to remember.

RICHARD ROHR

ONCE UPON A TIME, a young girl snuck into the hills behind her house where her secret friend was waiting for her. Snuck because her folks didn't like her running around the hills alone; they said it was dangerous. But she knew that her playmate created those hills and that danger was part of the wild adventures prepared for her. They shimmied around half-eroded paths, used tree roots as hand holds, and stole past herds of grazing bulls probably being fattened for the Tijuana bull ring.

Mostly, though, she lay in the tall grass making indentations just her size and felt her friend's breath against her face in the gentle breeze. And once, when this not-so-imaginary friend felt especially playful, a deer appeared in front of her, brought there for her enjoyment.

This is the God I first knew. Not because the Bible or the pastor (who happened to be my father) told me so, but because I knew from a delightful, secure knowledge deep within my being that I was loved. Wild adventures and breathtaking beauty were the agenda personally chosen for me, and no harm could come my way. This was a pure and intimate love with a Being greater and more beautiful than anything I could imagine and as real as anything I had ever known.

I knew from Sunday school this playmate of mine had been around for a very long time—indeed forever. I guess that made it all the more special, knowing this divine Being, who created the universe, was secretly waiting for me, beckoning me to come and play when I got home from school.

I grew up in Eden.

I remember "once upon a time" when everything in my little world seemed exactly as it should be. When good guys were good guys and bad guys were bad guys. We didn't know any bad guys but heard about them from time to time. They didn't live in our neighborhood.

INNOCENCE LOST

Ours was a close-knit community consisting of homes tucked against the hillside overlooking the city and the Pacific Ocean beyond. Each home belonged to people busy with life's responsibilities yet who always found time to wave and to share a greeting and homemade treats during the holidays.

The one exception was the house across the street. This house sat empty, the owners having vacated in a hurry. "Drugs," whispered a neighbor woman. "Running from the law." These words were spoken in hushed tones and piqued my brother's and my interest. Maybe the man who sold the home should have been suspicious when the "barefoot, hippie-types" paid for the house in cash.

You could feel the collective sigh in the air when the house was again occupied, this time by a man with curly red hair and a little red dog. We learned quickly that we'd have to forgive him for his less-than-neighborly manners, lowering the standards ever so slightly on our cul-de-sac, but at least there would be no more "barefoot, hippie-types" fleeing the neighborhood in front of our trusting eyes.

My brother Mark and I would wave as the man with curly red hair pulled into his driveway. Sometimes he'd wave back begrudgingly. We'd ask to pet his little red dog. He'd let us, again begrudgingly. Unfriendly, yes, but we figured it was nothing a batch of Mom's homemade pumpkin bread couldn't soften. When my brother and I got to his front door, the little dog began to bark. We waited . . . nothing. We knocked again. More barking, more waiting, two little children holding in their hands freshly baked bread wrapped by Mom with a smart red ribbon. Finally the door cracked open.

"Yes?"

"Mom baked some bread for you!" We peered around the door hoping to be invited in. He barked a "thanks" and quickly shooed us away.

Over the next months we tried to beat him down with our friendliness, greeting him with waves and smiles as he drove up the street or offering Girl Scout cookies at his door. We always received the same gruff response, if he came to the door at all.

We did not hear the screams the night our neighbor invited the stranger into his home. Mark and I were tucked safely into our beds a hundred or so feet away. With our bedtime stories read and prayers said, we were already dreaming of the adventures we'd have in the morning; we had no idea what was happening in the house across the street.

Our neighbor, it turns out, was committing murder.

In the days that followed, we began to overhear confusing messages spoken in low tones by adults or blurted out by the older neighbor kids: "Murder," and "Bulldozers sent into the hills searching for a shallow grave." It wasn't until years later that the story came together in bits and pieces. The body of a young woman was discovered in a ditch one town over and identified through dental records. The next owner of the home replaced the bloodstained carpet in the small bedroom facing the street. Apparently the man with curly red hair, besides being an unfriendly neighbor, had a propensity for killing people. He had invited a woman over to his house, a prostitute by trade, and taken her life with a baseball bat. And, we were told, years before he had done the same to someone else's daughter in someone else's hometown.

DISCOVERING BROKEN HALLELUJAHS

What happens when the harsh realities of life break into our safe places? What do we do when we discover things are not as they should be, when we realize life is no fairy tale and that pure, childlike belief in "happily ever after" turns into a cynical "sh— happens, deal with it"?

After I heard about the murder, I felt exposed and vulnerable, realizing for the first time that God and my parents might not always protect me. Fear crept in under the sheets. The world was a much more complicated place than I had thought.

I was being cast out of Eden.

I didn't know how to name the shifting landscape inside of me. It felt like the dissonant buzz and black and white fuzziness on the TV when we couldn't get a clear channel. I hated that buzz. With the dawning realization that the world was not the secure place I thought it was came the equally harrowing discovery that I had no idea what to do with the realities of death, disappointment, instability and fear. I had no idea how to live away from this garden home. I wasn't ready to leave. I hadn't packed my bags.

A New Sound of Music

The house across the street, besides holding a murderer, also held something else, something innocent and small.

Some years before the murder, long before the man with curly red hair moved in, that room held a crib with wooden bars and plastic covered rails. In that crib was a little girl standing on her tiptoes, peering over the rail in hopes that someone would hear her cries in the dark.

My first memory is standing in that crib. The bedroom that would later become a murder scene was my nursery. When my family first moved to Ventura, this was the home we settled into (and later moved across the street from). I was eighteen months old when we arrived, and my earliest memories of home formed within those walls.

The little bedroom was dark; night had fallen, but I was wide awake, unhappy. I remember the distress of feeling alone and longing for Mom or Dad to appear. Finally the door cracked open ushering in both the light of the hallway and the loving face of my father. As Dad picked me up I knew I was free, safe within his arms. Maybe he would take me down the hallway to their bedroom where I could snuggle between him and Mom in the Big Bed.

It is strange to think that this little geographical location holds someone's first memories and someone's last. It holds someone's cries that were met by her loving father and another's cries that went unheeded. How can anything hold such life and death, such light and darkness, such innocence and horror, such heaven and hell? This bedroom parallels the world I was being forcefully awakened to, and I've grown to understand it also mirrors my own heart.

Duality exists in me. Innocence and malevolence, intention and apathy, creativity and destructiveness, beauty and brokenness reign inside of me, as well as in my external environments. Can I find ways to hold this tension until it opens into something else, something expanding and softening instead of dulling and hardening? How can I honor the reality of brokenness without losing the memory and hope of wholeness? Where are my teachers?

I was discovering, even then as a young child, that if a hallelujah could be uttered out of the dark realities of life, it would be a "cold" and "broken" one. Death and a penetrating darkness entered into my awareness of what those hills held, a slow-motion shattering of my "happily ever after" ideology, making them alive with a more complex sound that I had not heard before. A sound incorporating notes of beauty and perfection right alongside those of death and devastation. A new song began playing, and with it began the initiation into a new journey, a journey of broken hallelujahs.

PRAYER PRACTICE: *Childhood Reflections*

Find a photograph or a series of photographs of you as a child. Invite God to journey with you in this reflection. (If you don't have a photograph, draw a picture of yourself as a child from your memory.)

Listen and engage. Take a few minutes to thoughtfully reflect on the child in the picture. Engage with this little person, allowing your thoughts and feelings to come. What do you see? What do you feel? Did this child experience a loss of innocence? Was there a time when all felt right with the world? Was there a time when all no longer felt right with the world? What were this child's first impressions of a divine being? Listen to your heart, remembering that the heart of the little child in the picture is your heart too. Acknowledge any hurts that might be present as you remember your childhood journey.

Connect. Have a spoken or written conversation with God (Jesus or the Spirit) about whatever has come up for you. You might ask

God to show you where God was present in your childhood. You might invite God into places of brokenness received in early life. Perhaps there are images of God you were given that have been damaging. You might ask God to highlight a place of truth and connection that reflected the reality of God's love in your early history. Let it flow. If possible, share what came up with a friend, spouse or small group.

two

Longing for Home

But trailing clouds of glory do we come
From God, who is our home.

WILLIAM WORDSWORTH

E VERY PART OF 2272 Hillcrest Drive is still vividly etched inside of me, from the treasured woodpile that would become go-carts and tree houses, to the cigar-smoking birds in top hats that, unbeknownst to our parents, my brother drew on the bamboo-patterned bathroom wall paper. I was five years old when we moved here from across the street. This was the house that provided the backdrop of my life until I left for college, and it continues to make welcome appearances in my dreams.

Mark and I would creep out of bed when we thought our parents were asleep and meet up in one of our bedrooms, usually his since it was the farthest away from our parents' room. He would regale me with historical stories about the making of the Statue of Liberty, adding jaw-dropping information like "Her little finger nail is bigger than that desk right there." Sometimes we would run up and down the hallway daring each other to touch our folks' bedroom door, occasionally with some type of streaking involved.

This is the house where Dad and I planted my first garden and where Mom taught me how to make my first batch of cookies. This is where I knelt, tying my shoes *without looking* as the deliveryman dropped off our first color TV. I was sure he noticed my accomplishment and was deeply impressed.

My brother and I spent hours building go-karts. Mark would meticulously design each vehicle, and I would get the thing built, proud of my ability to turn a pile of wood and two sets of old wheels into something we could jump on and race down the hill. In this home, under my parents' presence and protection, we were allowed to let our imaginations soar, free to create and test the limits of our abilities. I was loved, known and valued.

I realize that not everyone grows up in Eden, wrapped in such awareness. Many homes—most, perhaps—do not feel entirely safe and secure. All of us, I believe, have a God-given sense of what "home" feels like, what it should be: a place of safety, familiarity and acceptance. Home is where we leave pretense at the door, where we rest and connect.

In *Mere Christianity*, C. S. Lewis writes, "If I find in myself a desire which no experience in this world can satisfy, the most probable explanation is that I was made for another world." There is a homing mechanism deeply implanted in our souls, a restlessness leading us to our true home.

DISPLACEMENT

As children, all of us experience exile. At birth, we are cast out of a warm womb. For some, displacement is traumatic—the result of divorce, death or having to move from place to place. For others, it is more gradual. There are many ways to leave home.

Certainly the discovery that the man who lived across the street from us was a murderer and had killed a young woman in my former nursery created a sense of displacement in me; I could no longer live in my happy cocoon of naiveté. My home at 2272 Hillcrest Drive was the home where I loved and lost all my pets. With each loss, I learned that the things I love are not permanent. When my mom told me that her mother had died, I realized my parents could die too. I felt untethered and filled with a new kind of fear. I began to desperately pray that my parents would never leave me.

And this was the home where I grew more independent from my parents. No longer allowing myself to be rocked, held and healed by my mom's embraces. I learned that Mom's kisses and comfort did not make all pain go away or make my pets come back to life. I began to see that pain cannot be magically removed, but I had not yet learned that it must be suffered through. By nine or ten, I stopped letting her comfort me and companion me in the pain.

Further displacement came as I gravitated toward sports and found myself acculturated to the tough mentality of my teammates. Without meaning to, I internalized messages such as, "He cries *like a girl*" and "She throws *like a girl.*" I realized girls were thought to be weak and incompetent, things I did not want to be. I began a journey of exile from my own self as I no longer welcomed my own tears or feelings of vulnerability.

This was the home where Mark and I, as middle schoolers, began to grow distant. We grew to have almost nothing in common. I climbed trees and rode my Huffy dirt bike and *hated* having to come indoors when the streetlights came on. Mark spent more time holed up in his room reading or making illustrations and less time playing with his little sister. In high school, I played sports and had a group of good friends, a few of whom would be considered popular. Mark was in the marching band.

I felt the pain of displacement when my favorite youth pastor John resigned. He had loved me and taught me deep things about God. He saw beneath my silly, adolescent behaviors. He took my young life and faith seriously and taught me to do the same. I didn't know what to do with the pain, so I went on a run, and I ran until I was exhausted. This was the home I left behind as I began college life. People spoke of college as a great adventure filled with fun and freedom. I had no idea how lonely I would feel leaving behind everything I loved that was so familiar to me. My first year I drove the forty-five minutes back to my church every Sunday night for college group and the familiarity of my home and friends.

I didn't know how to deal with the abandonment I felt when my two best friends, who were also going to University of California at Santa Barbara, got an apartment together and created a new life for themselves without inviting me to be a part of it. My plan was, without knowing it, that they would provide the familiarity and stability needed to make a home in this new, foreign environment. We were ecstatic when we received our acceptance letters. We would be the three amigos, tackling this wild terrain with our usual humor and penchant for good, clean, slightly off-color fun. Instead, I sat in my dorm room across from my "Christian," "Non-smoking" roommate (the two boxes I had checked on the roommate preferences form) with whom I had next to nothing in common and felt a dark, creeping loneliness I had never felt before.

Wasn't college about fun and freedom, especially UC Santa Barbara? I sat silently in the dorm gatherings trying to understand the new social dynamics. Nobody knew me enough to get a kick out of Chango, my plaster-of-paris surf monkey proudly adopted from the Tijuana border. They just thought I was weird. I didn't know that transitions to good things, things I wanted and worked hard to achieve, could be so filled with loss.

I tried to find a faith community that would help me connect to God but found myself dodging anyone coming at me with too wide a smile. I longed for honest connection with others who were yearning, questioning and seeking God, but I grew disenchanted, believing the church was the last place I'd find it. Cynicism began to unpack its bags in my spirit, barring the door of church, so I'd sit at a coffee house, read Scripture and some Christian classic like A. W. Tozer or Teresa of Ávila, and alternate between feeling grateful for not having to deal with church dynamics and lonely.

I woke up to the painful realization that what church had meant to me—being at the center of a loving community—would probably never be repeated. I hadn't realized what a gift being a pastor's daughter had been; I had taken for granted how loved and cared for I was by so many.

While I was away at college, Dad put our house on the market. He needed to leave the church for health reasons, which meant saying goodbye to my tethers of security. I had assumed that family, home, neighborhood, church and hometown would always be there awaiting my return. Overnight all of this changed. So many places of loved geography lost, and the familiar faces who filled that geography also lost to me in a decision made beyond my control.

I felt alone and adrift.

Glimpses of Hope

We all have to leave places of familiarity, security and comfort. Often I am left longing to return. I want to go back in time, be with a certain person, feel the clarity and simplicity a certain time evokes, the comfort of that pet, the perfectness of that trip, the completeness I felt in that relationship. Instead of cynically squelching those "sentimental" feelings, I am trying to open to the longing underneath and explore how that longing can lead me in the present circumstance.

In each journey of leaving home, I discovered the "thin places" that allowed me to have the internal space necessary to open up in the midst of loss and loneliness. A "thin place" is a term that predates, but is commonly used in, Celtic spirituality to refer to places where the distance between heaven and earth seem gossamer thin, places where God feels especially close. In these places, my restless heart is rested and my longing for my true home is touched.

During college, these places came in the form of long nightly conversations with God along the cliffs of Isla Vista, staring at the ocean, discovering good books, working with developmentally disabled adults and new adventures with my brother. All these became places of connection and whiffs of heaven. The beauty, adventure and fun awaiting me began to be revealed as I settled into this new season.

I started to work summers at Forest Home, a Christian camp in the nearby mountains, where I became good friends with Laura. I also met a cute camp director named Joe. I couldn't have known at the time that these two people would become some of the most important ones in my life.

My last year of college, my brother Mark transferred to UCSB, and Mom began to send us letters with twenty dollar bills slipped inside. "Why don't you go out to eat together?" she would suggest. We did, and we realized we *liked* each other. These dinner dates are some of my favorite memories of college because it was then that Mark and I became friends.

Between my sophomore and junior years I moved from the dorms into a big house near the beach with good friends and created a fun home environment. It certainly wasn't Eden, but perhaps somewhere to the east, with a semblance of home.

If Eden is an image of true home, a biblical portrait of abundance, innocence, security and vulnerability, a place where we can be "naked and not ashamed," a place of deep connection to God, self, one another, animals and all of nature, then I think it's fair to say this side of heaven we are always slightly east, or west or south or north, of Eden. But we can get close enough from time to time to remember it's there, it's real, not just a place in fairy tales but a place in us that is awakened in fairy tales. It is the place where the Myth with a capital *M* lives, the place to which all other myths point. We come "from God, who is our home," and we are "trailing clouds of glory."

We all are homeless in one way or another at one time or another. "For Thou hast made us for Thyself and our hearts are restless till they rest in Thee," Augustine of Hippo reminds us. We all experience the restlessness of exile inherent in loss. And sometimes it takes a very long time to feel the realities of redemption, to experience the words of the psalmist, "God makes homes for the homeless" (Psalm 68:6 *The Message*).

Sometimes all we know is "we can't get there from here." All we can do is feel the ache of our restless hearts longing for home.

PRAYER PRACTICE: *Images of Home*

Listen to the homing mechanism deep inside of you.

What does *home* mean to you (a place of security, familiarity and belonging, or neglect, clutter, chaos and pain)?

When you think of a true home, what images come (a stuffed chair next to a warm fire, a grassy meadow, a full refrigerator, a loved one's embrace)?

What feelings come (longing, warmth, anger that your earthly home never felt like that, peaceful remembering)?

Are there places in you that feel at home?

Where are the places in you that do not feel at home? Where are you wandering through the wilderness, displaced and homeless?

In your places of homelessness, what image, ritual, music or person can you hold onto that means home for you? Is it enough to hold you until you can build a new home?

Engage. Draw, paint or create a poem or word picture around your image of home.

Connect. Talk with God about where God is providing for you in the areas of your homelessness. (Where is the manna in the wilderness?) Ask God to show you how God is leading you. (Where is the cloud by day and pillar of fire by night?) Ask God to reveal to you places of security, familiarity and belonging. Take a few minutes to feel and rest in the deeper image of home.

Listen and engage. Another suggestion is to find your "thin places," where heaven touches earth and God seems especially close. A monastery in the high desert of California is my thin place, as is my little church on Third and Ash in San Diego, the Beluga whales in a nearby aquarium, favorite playgrounds with my kids, the shoreline where I surf, a couple favorite coffee houses and our deck at sunset. In each of these places I feel like I have come home. Find your thin places. Go to them as often as you are able, physically or mentally. In times of loss, be sure to spend time in these places.

Connect. Thin places connect us to God through our bodies and environment. Words are not necessary. Simply sit, rest, be.

- three -

Love and Disillusionment

The course of true love never did run smooth.

WILLIAM SHAKESPEARE,
A Midsummer Night's Dream

I AM SLOW TO FALL IN LOVE. Never have I experienced anything close to "love at first sight." All through high school, I would much rather hang out with my friends than date. Dating always seemed to involve some kind of pretense and uncomfortable shoes.

But while working at summer camp, living in community and donning the most comfortable, well-worn hiking boots, I fell hard for the cute camp director named Joe. After a sweet and semi-innocent romance, we decided to "date" from afar as he went back to school near Chicago and I returned to Santa Barbara.

The next summer I returned to camp along with my "boyfriend," excited to see where the romance would go. It went nowhere, and I was deeply hurt and confused. *Weren't we perfect for each other?* I thought our feelings were reciprocal. He's the one who pursued dating, who suggested we continue from a distance, who said amazingly vulnerable things to me that he would only say, I believed, if he *really loved* me.

I was shattered. A new place had come to life inside of me with this relationship, or perhaps a long forgotten place had come back to life, and now I wished it hadn't. The scent of Eden had stayed with me longer than most, but now my memories seemed like a cruel trick, making reality all the more painful. The expulsion from the garden was complete. The angels stood fast, barring my return. And I felt ridiculous believing any of that tender garden, that innocent love, was true.

I remember the numb feeling of those days. I didn't know what to do with my longings. I didn't understand that I would not always feel that way, that new life would come. I hadn't yet learned that death comes in the middle and not the end of the story. I just felt dead.

In an ironic twist of fate—or maybe it was God's wily ways—that cute camp director was the man standing in front of the church awaiting me as I walked down the aisle ten years later. It is a deeply satisfying thing when the one who has broken your heart is the one who helps put those pieces back together again. We had done a lot of growing up in our twenties and reconnected six years after taking one another off the list of potential life partners.

Joe and I have come to believe that any good relationship should begin with a thorough and complete break up. We both thought there was no way we would marry each other, so we had the freedom to develop a deep and honest relationship.

PLAYING BY THE RULES

In third grade, under my new friend Felicia's influence, I got a pass and met her in the girls' bathroom, where we wrote the naughtiest word we knew in pencil across the bathroom wall. This word, which predates and was used by Shakespeare, is what my son would say loudly at three years old when trying to say "truck."

I remember having to call my mom to tell her I would miss the bus because I had to stay after school. I remember sitting in the principal's office. I wasn't quite sure why I did it other then Felicia encouraged me and it felt kind of fun being naughty. I wondered if this was the kind of person I was becoming, one of those naughty kinds of people. But my "life of crime" was to stop at lightly defacing the bathroom wall *in pencil*. Weak, I know. My testimony has always been wanting.

I have discovered that I like playing by the rules more than I like breaking them and suffering the consequences. My personality is such that I like being good. My mother fondly remembers over-hearing a conversation I had with the neighbor girl who had in-quired about my denominational affiliation. At four years old I con-fidently told her, "I'm not a Presbyterian"—believing such a complicated word must be naughty—"I'm a good girl!" Mom couldn't wait to tell Dad, my Presbyterian pastor father.

In marriage, I have learned that there are different sets of rules, and I like playing by mine. Family systems and personality types have embedded completely different sets of rules into my husband's and my DNA. Who knew? I have also learned that my preference to "play by the rules" is less about me being a "good girl" and more about my core need to feel secure. I like very much when one plus two equals three and not so much when one plus two equals *n* or some such algebraic nonsense.

While others are performing dastardly acts of courageous wrong-doing, I shimmy along at my subtle attempts of security main-tenance. Honestly, most days, I'd rather have a stable marriage, happy kids, secure finances, good health and a few good waves than a Savior. Particularly a Savior who beckons me to follow him, caring nothing if my ducks are all in a row. "Do you not care that we are perishing?" cried the disciples in a boat filling with water, and they were, by the way, in all likelihood perishing. "Why are you afraid? Have you still no faith?" Jesus says.

Really, Jesus? I'll tell you why, it's because they were drowning! Water was filling the boat and they had no former walking-on-water experience to go on. And also because plenty of people who believe in you drown, including the missionary I heard about who was eaten by a shark while swimming in the tropical waters of the country he believed you called him to.

Yeah, security is a biggie for me.

If I'm going to follow someone, give my life to them and all, I want to be sure that everything is going to turn out okay, and I don't mean solely on an eternal level. Same with marriage. So I paid due diligence. I prayed, I shopped around a bit, and I didn't jump at the first shiny thing that caught my eye. It took ten years! We had the support of our families and communities, we went to counseling, and I believed we were ready for a steady and stable marriage until death do us part. This is not, I have discovered, the way marriage works.

I know what I said in the wedding ceremony, it's on video, for goodness sake: "For better or *for worse*, in *sickness* and in health . . ." But really, it's only when things got worse that I realized I didn't really mean it. I wasn't aware until the sickness part set in that I thought marriage was something that would make my life easier. I thought I would have someone to talk to, share my emotional hardships with and help pay the bills. Sometimes marriage makes my life worse, and I say this fully loving my husband, grateful for him and believing I made the right choice.

I am not easy to be married to. The line taken from an old Scots-Irish prayer could have been written for me: "Lord, grant that I may always be right, for Thou knowest I am hard to turn." Joe calls this my righteous indignation mode. It took a tattoo being permanently etched into my skin to turn around my judgmental attitude toward my neighbors who ran the tattoo parlor. And putting my need for security and ease slightly above the rigors of marriage is problematic: the outcome is frequent disappointment and disillusionment.

Joe does not always play by the rules I want him to play by, the subtler ones I thought we were in agreement on when we said, "I do." In many ways I can say the same thing about my journey of faith. God does not play by my rules or the neat constructs of my mental understandings. Joe and Jesus do not always seem to care about my need for security and ease, as it turns out; they both have agendas of their own. Sometimes my marriage stretches me further than I want to be stretched, and I have a feeling this is by design.

LOSING ENCHANTMENT

Single life was brutal in a culture so couple-centric; it was tough for me to stay tender while trying to navigate the dating scene. Once married, I reasoned, my heart and body would be able to relax in the safe and stable environment of love. This has been partially true; places inside me have been healed, deep cynicism washed away. However, I didn't anticipate the distancing and hardening that would also be a result of marriage.

In times of stress, come to find out, Joe and I "reverse" each other, to use the perfect psychological term. I go into fight mode, Joe freezes. The more I fight, the more Joe shuts down. The more Joe shuts down, the more my anxiety rises and I want to fight.

Maybe it was those "Christian" books that led me to believe in a "happily ever after" if we did things the "right" way. We get married, grow together in intimacy and ease, complete each other's sentences, then sit hand in hand on our porch swing watching the grandkids play at our feet, right? I remember the first time I took Joe to the monastery I love; he addictively worked on his crossword puzzle with this trapped animal look on his face. This set off a series of panic buttons in me: I need silence, he needs noise. I need stillness, he needs constant activity, and so on.

The story of our marriage doesn't fit into the pages of any of these books, particularly in stressful times, which seem to be somewhat continuous. I wish those books had said, "the love that consists in this: that two solitudes protect, and border, and greet each other," as poet Rainer Maria Rilke knew. Of course, if I had read this in my younger days, I probably would have said, "Whatever."

I will say that marriage has been the greatest vehicle of spiritual formation in my life. It is in marriage that my false self appears, my false belief systems, my desires, needs, dependencies, all the broken stuff inside, the wounded places, the critical voices, the unconscious expectations. There is no hiding, no running back into my private life where I once believed I was a kind, flexible and nice person. I am discovering that "love is not a victory march," as Leonard Cohen sings.

In marriage I am trying to choose vulnerability, even though it will lead to a broken heart from time to time. I am learning to love and be loved in ways that aren't always natural and intuitive to me but are real just the same. Marriage is helping me recognize how much I see others through my own distortions. The act of seeing, Anthony De Mello tells us, is "the most painful act the human being can perform," because it forces us to confront our tendencies to see the other through our desires, memories, imaginations and projections. I am striving to see Joe beyond my fears and projections, to grow to love him in his otherness.

Maybe someday I'll title my marriage book *How to Marry Just a Guy.* This is so much better than *How to Marry Your Soulmate: The One Who Will Complete You and Satisfy Your Every Need.* The latter will no doubt out-sell the former. But if I could learn how to be married to "just a guy," and help others do the same, maybe more of us would have a chance of succeeding in this crazy, courageous commitment of lifelong union, and in doing so, we might just see the divine seeping through our beloved's guyness (or galness).

PRAYER PRACTICE: *Opening Clenched Fists*

Listen. Prayerfully ask God to bring to mind your relational journeys. Are there people and situations you are holding on to that you are being invited to release into God's hands? Are there fears and worries you are holding on to? Are there hopes and dreams you are clinging to too tightly? Are there things you need to forgive others for? What do you need to forgive yourself for? Are there failures or expectations that you have not met? Do you need to forgive God for not providing or protecting you in ways you believed God would?

Engage. Write down what comes on small, separate pieces of paper. As you hold each piece, let yourself experience the emotions, thoughts and memories that come as you reflect on what you wrote, then hold the paper tightly in your clenched fist.

Connect. Listen to the words of Henri Nouwen from *With Open Hands,* and as you do, allow God to pry open your clenched fist and release what you are holding to God as best as you can.

> Don't be afraid to offer your hate, bitterness, disappointment, to the One who is love and only love. . . . Each time you dare to let go and surrender . . . your hand opens a little and your palms spread out in a gesture of receiving. You must be patient, of course, very patient, until your hands are completely open.

Forgiving ourselves and others, releasing our fears, failures and painful situations along with anything else good or bad we are clinging to, is usually not a one-time thing. We are affected by these things in so many ways. Don't be discouraged if one event or reaction keeps coming up after you have prayed. Instead, trust that if something is disturbing your spirit, there is simply more there to give to God and you get another opportunity to practice releasing. This is a muscle worthy of exercising.

You may burn or rip up and throw away the paper as a means of further release.

- four -

Losing My Strength

Sickness is more instructive than
a long trip to Europe.

FLANNERY O'CONNOR

HAD SOMEONE TAKEN A SNAPSHOT at that moment, it would have shown a young woman sitting in a wheelchair watching her husband stick a needle in his gut. Behind them loomed the towering launch pad at Kennedy Space Center. People passing by might have concluded we were attempting some drug-induced space travel of our own, when in reality, my husband simply wanted to eat a sandwich.

Three years prior, I had walked down the aisle in a tight, sequined, sleeveless wedding gown, the small bruise appearing on my upper arm, a happy reminder of the pre-marital surf I had taken with my bridesmaid that morning. I walked arm in arm with my father in a joy-induced daze, drawn forward by the smiling, radiant gaze emanating from my soon-to-be husband's face. He was literally glowing; people said I was too. A cherished snapshot forever etched in my mind.

In the imaginary snapshot at Kennedy Space Center where we sat wilting in the Florida humidity, I watched my husband prick his finger and carefully place the tiny drop of blood on a test strip. He did this three times before the meter blinked, able to read his blood sugar level. A few seconds later, a number appeared: 81. "Okay, let's see, that's on the low side of normal." Now he looked at his lunch and tried to figure out which parts of the ham and cheese sandwich had carbohydrates and how many carbs they might contain. Then out came the vial of insulin, needle and antiseptic wipe. Five minutes later, he finally took his first bite of sandwich just as I had completed my last.

How did we get here?

I found myself looking at us through the eyes of an elderly couple that walked by and allowed myself to feel some of the sympathy I saw in their eyes. Type 1 diabetes arrived, uninvited, into Joe's story two years into our marriage. One year before Joe's diagnosis, while I was training for a bicycle pilgrimage across Spain, the abrupt and confusing onset of arthritis entered into my story and refused to leave. Almost overnight I went from being an athlete to being the person hanging the blue handicap placard on her car. Physical therapy, injections, acupuncture, diet changes, medications and surgery—nothing seemed to help. What does it mean to be an athlete who can't walk or stand without discomfort?

WHO AM I?

When a part of our body is hurting or doesn't work the way it has in the past, it's like having a dependent child who requires constant attention. With arthritis, a whole new set of questions entered my world, a whole new kind of planning. My body used to do things automatically but with the onset of arthritis I had to think, *What shoes will I wear to go shopping? Will I need my knee braces and walking sticks to take this hike? Are there benches at the museum? A wheelchair available at the amusement park?* And everyone had something to try to make my arthritis disappear. Stop eating tomatoes. Go to this healing prayer service. Try acupuncture. Take glucosamine.

How do I navigate this confusing, new world? Who do I listen to?

In most of the real and imaginary snapshots taken during the first few years of marriage, we look like you might expect. We talked, we laughed, we were affectionate, we argued, we explored new places together. But underneath the surface, two new journeys had begun.

In one, I was journeying with a husband who was young and handsome but no longer as invincible as I had believed. I began carrying sugar tablets in my backpack and cake frosting in my car, not in preparation for an impromptu cake decorating party, but so I might be able to save my husband's life if he dropped into a diabetic coma.

Our bodies had let us down. Life felt vulnerable, fragile and without the physical assurances I had counted on and assumed would remain reliable in young bodies.

I grappled with deep questions of identity. I had been an athlete, lettering in high school and completely "stoked," as they say, with my ability to walk on water. Almost thirty years into the sport, I still find surfing miraculous. It is my way of stepping out of the boat, Peter-like, of being beckoned by something greater than myself to engage directly in the elements of creation. I surf with people of all ages, including an octogenarian or two, and I assumed I too would be surfing well into my golden years. After the onset of arthritis I wondered how long I had in the water.

What about children? I wondered. Didn't we hear that diabetes has a genetic component? And what about my arthritis? The onset was so fast; if this pace of deterioration continues, I won't be walking for much longer. Will I be able to chase little ones around the house? Can I keep them from darting in front of cars if I can't dart myself?

Loving Our Bodies

Grieving always involves love. We can't grieve until we are able to recognize our love for what is lost. Then comes the process of learning to love what remains, as imperfect as it may be. I don't know many people who deeply love their body. I know of plenty of people who don't like their body and plenty who obsess over it, but to tenderly love these bundles of flesh and bones like we love our children is so rare. How many of us can see a snapshot or look in the mirror at our real bodies and smile tenderly at what we see, scars, lumps and all?

Here's the thing about snapshots: they lie. Okay, maybe *lie* is a bit strong. The click of a camera captures a moment frozen in time, and frozen moments can never tell the whole story. That's why the midst of crisis is not time to make big decisions; snapshots reveal partial truth at best.

There is no such thing as a frozen moment, only movement and change. I have often heard it said that the one thing we can count on in life is change. For someone who *really* likes predictability, inconsistency as the only constant is not a comforting thought, though it certainly rings true. Emerson said, "People wish to be settled; only as far as they are unsettled is there any hope for them." God bless him, but I hate this.

Just because a snapshot of something like a car accident or cancer diagnosis grabs our attention more quickly than the myriad of beautiful snapshots, the ones that show us laughing, living, loving, doesn't mean they are more real. They are not. Many things in life actually get better, including some of the most difficult things like intense loss, loneliness and failure. There is always more life to be had, more beauty to be discovered, more love to be given and received.

Happily, my arthritis and Joe's diabetes are both playing out in ways that are much better than we had envisioned. Joe has not once dropped into a diabetic coma, and I no longer carry cake frosting around. We have had some significant ups and downs with Joe's diabetes, but the last down led him to commit to daily exercise, something he never imagined he could do, and a decision that has encouraged me in my own pursuit of health. I see the boost of confidence and vitality exercise brings to both of us.

And my knees are strong enough to get me almost everyplace I want to go. I continue to learn to love my body, broken as it is, and to love what it has allowed me to do and who it has allowed me to hold, carry and love.

PRAYER PRACTICE: *Take a Bath*

Draw a warm bath, light a candle, soak, let go and breathe. (I light a candle for ambiance and to not notice the dirty grout vying for my attention.)

Breathe in the warmth of God's love and breathe out in words, or simply in the silence of your breath, all the heaviness you are holding in your body and mind.

If we don't ever notice what our bodies are holding and feeling, how can we heal from loss? Our bodies don't lie; they simply experience what they experience. Remember, your body is sacred; it is the temple of the Holy Spirit. What parts of your body feel at peace? What parts need your attention? Rest and breathe. Are you fighting against the thoughts *This is a waste of time; I've got more important things to do*? Many of us so quickly dismiss or ignore our physical needs. If this is you, ask yourself, *why?* Where in your body do you hold your emotional tensions? Where do you hold fear, anxiety, anger? If you notice areas of discomfort, invite God's touch.

Listen to your body.

Engage your aches and pains, tensions and tender areas as you soak in warm water.

Connect with your body. Our body connects us to the present moment. Allow yourself to feel held and tenderly surrounded as you rest and release into God's presence through the warm water. Practice loving this sacred temple.

Time disappears in water, and a ten-minute bath can be just the retreat needed.

- five -

Longing for a Child

First comes love, then comes marriage,
then comes baby in a baby carriage.

PLAYGROUND SONG

WHEN I BECAME SUSPICIOUS that a baby might be starting a life within me, Joe and I were about to leave for a weekend away to Julian, California, a tiny, historic mountain community famous for its apple pie. After we settled into our bed and breakfast, I took a pregnancy test I had secretly slipped into my bag. I read the packaging three times before believing that two solid lines meant my hunch was confirmed. I was pregnant.

I set the test on the windowsill and suggested Joe check out the view, which he did and became very interested in the old buildings across the street. After numerous attempts to try to subtly redirect my ADHD husband's gaze toward the awaiting test, I finally pointed directly at it and said, "Oh look, what's this?" Joe looked at it intently having no idea what two lines meant. I handed him the paper. "Oh my gosh! Really? We're pregnant?!"

The timing couldn't have been better. We had learned that type 1 diabetes has a very little, if any, genetic component. And as far as my arthritis was going, things had not deteriorated. We had recently returned from traveling around the country, were settling into our new home—a great old loft in downtown San Diego—had become financially stable and were now ready to welcome a little person into our lives. We spent the rest of the weekend hand in hand, talking about our future dreams, exploring our favorite used bookstore and the old pioneer cemetery on the hill, window shopping, eating apple pie with the crumbly crust topping, talking about nothing at all and sipping coffee from thick mugs, all the while harboring a wonderful secret.

One month later, I walked through the gnarled oaks in San Diego's Balboa Park harboring another kind of secret. The baby had not grown. A "blighted ovum" were the words the doctor used, words that floated around the room, bumping into the sterile, pastel walls. Instead of finding a growing baby, my first pregnancy ultrasound had found an eleven-centimeter tumor growing in my abdomen.

Everything slowed down as I watched more words curiously bouncing around the room, not landing. Oddly, in this slow-motion revelation of very bad news, my body felt somewhat euphoric. Something big has just been revealed, my brain was telling me, that will affect the rest of my life.

Over the next few days, the adrenaline rush, perhaps a gift our bodies give to help us handle devastating news, had begun to dissipate. As I walked through the park, I was trying to process the idea of not having children. I was also trying to process the possibility that I might have something inside of me that could take my life.

My mom had been diagnosed with breast cancer at seventy years of age, had endured a double lumpectomy, chemo and radiation all while working full time for a San Diego hospice. I remember hearing statistics about cancer in high school. At nineteen, when one of our gang got cancer, I believed that, statistically, the rest of us should be okay. The same magical thinking played out in my mind knowing that my mom had battled cancer. If I also have cancer, that's statistically unfeasible, and children are not supposed to die before their parents. Fortunately, I had planned this time to process right before a scheduled meeting with my spiritual director. Chris sat with me and listened, her face glowing with compassion and concern. She offered very little in the way of advice. Instead she gave me her physical presence, and with it came the very concrete reminder of God's presence.

The surgery revealed a benign tumor that would not impede further pregnancy. Hallelujah! Joe and I and my entire family breathed out a long, slow sigh of relief. God had healed my mom and healed me. The psalmist in Psalm 113 proclaims, "[The Lord] gives the childless wife a home, the joyful mother of children. Hallelujah!" (v. 9 NAB).

Thanks be to God!

And now, let's have a baby.

WHEN THE EXPECTED DOESN'T HAPPEN

I never know what expectations I am holding until they either violently shatter or slowly get pecked to death by the chickens of fate. When what I thought was a violent shattering of our dreams of children from the tumor diagnosis and miscarriage turned out to be a false alarm, I assumed pregnancy would naturally follow. We had gone through the wilderness and were ready to enter the Promised Land. I was not prepared for the pecking that was to come.

Two years later, still childless, we decided to pursue fertility options. We were poked, prodded, tested and diagnosed. It didn't look good. In vitro fertilization, the most invasive, unnatural, expensive way to have a baby was our only option, we were told. I remember giving a report in fifth grade on the first "test-tube" baby amid giggles and shocked expressions of disbelief. And now, I was going to try to have a baby that was put together on a petri dish by some guy in a lab?

After much thought and prayer, we decided to begin the process. Our first attempt failed after months of injections, surgery and a nearly depleted bank account. Our family encouraged us to continue and helped with the medical bills. Our second attempt was successful, and I became pregnant.

Three months later, after a routine ultrasound, we left the doctor's office in silence and walked among twisted, wind-battered trees on the La Jolla coast trying to grasp the words we had just heard: "I am so sorry, the embryo has stopped growing, the pregnancy has ended." After three months of living with the ecstatic belief that our dream had come true and that God had answered our prayers, our baby died.

Another surgery to remove another lost pregnancy. Joe sat in the waiting room during the operation, distracting himself as best he could with magazines. As I was going under, I felt the cessation of all emotional and physical pain for a few precious seconds, such a stark contrast to all I had been feeling and would wake to feel again. A few hours later, he took me home, put me into bed and lovingly tended to my needs, as internally we began withdrawing into our separate corners of grief.

I had always assumed that children would be part of my life. I had no idea how complicated the whole getting pregnant thing could be.

We returned to Julian that winter, the same town where I'd learned about my first pregnancy. The trip there was marked by a ridiculous argument that left me utterly unsympathetic about Joe's dropping blood sugar level. The argument was one of many that seemed to come out of the blue, having no discernible trigger other than the grief we were both harboring. I took a nap and woke up a better person. Joe found some sugar and forgave me.

We read and rested, went to our favorite Italian restaurant, wandered leisurely through the used bookstore and ended up at the Julian Pioneer Cemetery, in the garden of the innocents, surrounded by graves of little ones lost way before anyone was ready to let them go. We huddled side by side on a bench beneath scraggly, winter-wasted trees surrounded by yellow grass and mud. We held hands under the gray, silent sky.

A time of distancing set in. Slowly, subtly, I began distancing myself from my longings to become a mother and from the hurt this journey was creating. I did not want to keep waiting for a future yet to be determined. I also began distancing myself from the God who refused to answer the question I desperately wanted to know the answer to, namely, "Will I ever be a mother?"

That same winter, I spent a few days at St. Andrew's Abbey, a monastery I love in the high desert of California. I wanted to get in touch with my own heart and with the God who had grown silent. But I found myself unable to pray, even in this safe and sacred place. I wandered down to the monastery bookstore looking for some distraction. I stumbled upon a sculpture of a father with his infant child playfully draped around his shoulders. The image opened up a deep place of grief inside of me for my husband. I wasn't able to access such grief for my own loss. I wondered, *What if Joe is never able to be a father?* In that bookstore the hidden longing in my heart broke through. I collapsed into a nearby chair and cradled the image in my hands as the tears flowed down my cheeks.

LIVING IN HOLY SATURDAY

The next day I briefly shared some of my struggles with Father Francis, a jovial, kind and profound soul, and former abbot of the monastery. He handed me a book that talked about how our journeys of waiting and unfulfillment are necessary if we desire to find our fulfillment in God. "Holy Saturday, which falls between

Good Friday and Easter Sunday in the church calendar, is the day the church recognizes unfulfillment and waiting," he explained. He encouraged me to enter into the story with the apostles and to recognize that Holy Saturday is an important part of our journey. Christ had died, along with their dreams of salvation. They huddled together and hoped beyond hope that the impossible would happen, that Christ would rise again.

For Christians, much of life on earth is lived on Holy Saturday. We are no longer in Eden, and our heavenly homecoming is yet to be realized. We are living in an unfinished symphony. The resurrection reality breaks into our world by many "secret touchings," as Julian of Norwich reminds us, and yet we are left "still longing for love" until the day that we die.

Waiting is hard.

After my visit to the monastery, I began to conscientiously grieve the possibility of not having a child. On a few occasions I suggested we look into adoption. Joe was not open to the idea, feeling a deep desire to have his Russian bloodline continue. Before I started another round of in vitro I needed to come to terms with a God who might not give me "the desires of my heart"—at least not in the way I once believed God would, not in the way I wanted. I needed to be able to say yes to God, regardless of the outcome. Eventually the words formed inside of me, the Holy Spirit's work, no doubt: "Yes, Lord, I am yours regardless of whether I am to be a mother or not."

On our last attempt at in vitro fertilization, I became pregnant. As time progressed and I began to believe in the viability of this pregnancy, I began to prepare for the life that was to come. I decided to conscientiously address the parts of my life I would be losing with this incredible gain. I journaled about the loss of free time and the decrease in intimacy with my husband and with God. When I birthed our healthy baby girl, what I wasn't prepared for was the overwhelming scent of Eden that came back into my world with her arrival.

Seventeen months later her little brother was born. We are still trying to figure out how this happened. They truly arrived "trailing clouds of glory," to use Wordsworth's line. It felt to me as if they had been in God's womb before they entered mine; everything about them reminded me of heavenly places long forgotten. Now I watch as my kisses magically make the pain of a skinned knee go away and I remember something of the truths underneath the fairy tales. I hadn't realized how shallow my breathing had become until I sucked in that long-forgotten sense of true home that came in through their eyes and skin and scent.

Sometimes dreams do come true, sometimes Eden is not just a distant memory, sometimes the stories we live in here and now are resurrection stories. Sometimes we hear God speaking to us as he spoke to Julian of Norwich, "I can make all things well, and I shall make all things well, and I will make all things well; and you will see yourself, that every kind of thing will be well."

And sometimes, even when the endings to our stories aren't as happy as my journey into motherhood, we believe it.

PRAYER PRACTICE:
Good Friday, Holy Saturday, Easter Sunday

Multiple stories are playing out in our lives at the same time. How do we hold and honor such varying experiences? Christ's journey and the liturgical writings and practices of Holy Week can help hold the stories present in the human experience.

Listen. Where are you living in Good Friday? These are the places inside of you and in your circumstances where death and darkness reign. Hope is not present, and expectations are shattered. These are the places where life is not as you hoped it would be.

Where are you living in Holy Saturday? These are the places of waiting, where the results are unknown and you can't force things to happen. Where you are powerless to influence how the story will play out. Where do you long for healing, wholeness and consummation?

Where are you living in Easter Sunday? These are the resurrection realities in and around you, where you feel loved and at home. Where are you experiencing beauty, joy, healing, wholeness and consummation? Sometimes it's hard to stop and notice when your body or your relationships or your kids or finances are doing well. Stop and listen.

Engage by writing down or sketching, perhaps in a stream-of-consciousness fashion, words or images that come.

Connect by having a conversation with God and a friend, spouse or small group about your thoughts and feelings regarding what you noticed.

A suggestion for deepening the experience: choose one of the situations above and ask if you are open to listening to this part of yourself. If so, take a few moments to create a loving environment where you have some uninterrupted time and space to listen deeply to your heart. Then let yourself drop down into the feelings that surround this situation. Perhaps you feel a weight on your shoulders, an ache in your gut or a fluttering in your chest. Surround this feeling with love and see if it wants to reveal anything. Perhaps an image or word comes. Listen tenderly to this part of you, as you would to a child who needs you and wants to tell you something. Don't try to change or fix it; just listen and ask Jesus to come help you care for this part of you.

SIX

Losing My Brother

Grieving is the process of accepting the unacceptable.

FATHER ISAAC, Saint Andrew's Abbey,
quoting the well-known adage

MOM GREETED ME AT MY front door as I came in from my morning surf session. She had been watching her new granddaughter, my three-month-old Allena, when the call came. "They found an eight-centimeter tumor in Mark's brain," she said.

Still dripping with salt water, my brain struggled to register what she was telling me.

It was impossible to believe. Eight centimeters—that's the size of an orange! My brother was the healthiest, most active person I knew. He was the one who climbed ten-thousand-foot peaks on a whim in his Converse hightops. He's the one who said, "Mom, I think I'll bike to school," meaning his college four hundred miles away. He'd just completed writing a beautiful, scholarly book for the San Diego Maritime Museum. (You can't do that with a quarter of your brain taken away by a tumor, can you?) I didn't even know he had been feeling dizzy, seen a doctor or had an MRI. How could he *not* be fine?

Within the hour, Mark and Laura, his wife and one of my best friends since we met so many years ago at the same camp where I met Joe, were sitting at my parents' kitchen table. They told us all they knew, details that would change our lives forever.

That evening Mark asked if we could take a walk. As we strolled around his neighborhood Mark told me that he could be gone in two years. "I have no regrets," he said, "and the idea of dying doesn't scare me, but the thought of leaving Laura and the boys behind, that's hard." We walked together in silence. Every crack in the concrete came alive as my brain surged with emotions.

Three years later Mark and I would walk around this same block again, his right foot slapping the ground as he shuffled precariously forward. I readied myself to catch him, knowing I couldn't manage his now one-hundred-pound heavier frame. Brain surgery, brain herniation, strokes and irreparable damage, one sad story after another, had been the rabbit-hole journey we'd all fallen into.

On this walk, like many others before it, Mark brought up the loss of his bicycle, the same one he rode to school so many years ago. He rode it someplace when he was still able to ride, then could not remember where he left it. Mark had lost so much during these past three years since his cancer diagnosis: his short-term memory, his ability to work, drive or carry on any semblance of the active, productive life he once knew. But the thing he came back to time and time again was the loss of his beloved bicycle.

"I think God is a bicycle thief," I told him after the thought snuck into my head. He looked at me as if I was the one with brain damage. "I'm serious," I assured him. "What if God took your bike to prepare your home for you? I mean, doesn't that make sense? Pearly gates and streets of gold don't sound all that appealing, but your beloved bicycle waiting for you to explore your new home? I wouldn't put it past God, would you?"

Mark, who had recently been placed on hospice and given six months to live, paused to take in what I was saying. Out of breath, exhausted from our short walk around the block, he smiled. "I like that," he said.

TIGHT SPOTS

Mark had a long history of getting himself out of tight spots. More than once I was the recipient of this uncanny ability of his. We all believed cancer would be no different, that he would somehow make it through, with God's help.

In our twenties, Mark and I became avid Baja travelers. We'd bring whatever vehicle we had deep into the Baja interior. On one trip we became hopelessly lost looking for some mission ruins. Night was descending and we were off the map on jeep tracks hours away from human life, a road that probably hadn't been traveled on for months. I began to panic and remember the stories of people lost in the Baja desert never to return. Mark thought it was fun.

"Just wait, it will be okay," he said. "These roads have to lead somewhere."

We chose one and an hour later ended up at the home of a hardy ranchero and his equally hardy wife who welcomed us with coffee, homemade cheese, a place to spend the night and directions to the mission ruins. We sat in their kitchen talking long into the night in our broken Spanish, Mark's face aglow in the kerosene lantern.

I remember one "expedition" where we found ourselves creeping up a steep grade on very tilted jeep tracks. Mark calmly suggested I open the door and hang out as far as possible to provide a counterweight as he tried to keep the highly tippable Suzuki Samurai on the path that cut precariously along a mountainside. I did, and once again, we lived to tell the tale.

One of my favorite memories was the weekend before I was to have knee surgery. Joe and I had been married for a couple of years, and I had received my arthritis diagnosis. The surgery was going to clean up some loose, deteriorating cartilage that was possibly leading to my knee pain. I could barely walk but decided it would be a good time to do one of our long-imagined sibling adventures: to drive ten hours down the peninsula to Bahia de Los Angeles, kayak out to the deserted desert islands and camp. Laura, Mark's wife, was *very* pregnant at the time with their first child. What were we thinking?!

We pulled into the bay late at night and slept lightly under the stars in anticipation of the adventures ahead. The next morning Mark helped me hobble into my kayak, and off we went for a five-mile paddle to the desolate islands. We set up camp and Mark went exploring as I read, trying to use my knees as little as possible. We were completely on our own: no other human beings, no signs of civilization and no communication devices.

The night before we were to paddle back to civilization we could feel a change in the air. This could be the Santa Ana winds coming, we reasoned. I felt my anxiety rise. These winds can be incredibly dangerous. Darkness crept into my spirit as I thought about the possibility of not making it back for my surgery and tried not to think about the possibility of not making it back at all.

"Beth, look!" Mark interrupted my thoughts. He pointed to a light streak coming from the water. I could see nothing but my fear of an unknown future as Mark sat overwhelmed by the beauty of it all. Then I saw a burst of light. *What on earth?* I thought. More lights began bursting beneath the surface of the water. Were we watching the reflection of a shower of shooting stars? Or had someone dropped a bucket of flashlights into the water? Tiny bioluminescent marine plankton were lighting up the sea. It reminded me of the first time Mark and I discovered lighting bugs as kids on a family vacation to the Midwest. We could not believe the magical bursts of light were being produced by bugs.

"Beth, we'll be okay," he reassured me. "We don't know about tomorrow, but look at what we get to see tonight. We are the only two people here to see this, just you and me."

We jumped into our kayaks for a midnight paddle and discovered that the microscopic creatures were activated by movement. The bursts of luminescence they emitted formed a surreal display of light. Light above us, shining down from millions of unobstructed stars, and light underneath us, bursting in the wake of paddle pull and darting fish. A breathtaking show for the two of us alone to enjoy.

I let Mark persuade me to engage deeply in the present moment and experienced one of the most magical nights of my life.

The glow of the night's adventures still surging through our sleeping minds ended abruptly when our little tent began heaving in the wind. The Santa Anas had arrived, making our planned paddle back to the mainland impossible. We had been warned of the dangers, so we had carried an extra day's worth of water and food. I sat on the beach and slipped back into worry as Mark happily climbed the island's highest peak in his ever-present black hightops. I watched the tiny speck of my brother ascending the rocky slope and knew he was fully enjoying himself. Eventually I gave up worrying and looked around. I took a deep breath, inviting the beauty into my anxiety, then felt the invitation to jump in. I scooted myself seal-like into the water for a little snorkeling, then lay on my back and floated. I let the water hold me.

Toward midday the winds died down a bit, and we decided to try a crossing. It took all my strength and was more than my muscles could handle. I ended up with pulled muscles in both wrists, but together we made it to safety.

We had made it out of yet another tight spot with new memories and new stories to tell, my invincible brother and me.

A MIRACLE

Mark was wheeled into surgery two weeks after the tumor was discovered. Joe and I were scheduled to be working in Atlanta two thousand miles away. Joe went and covered all of my responsibilities and his so that I could be where I needed to be: huddled with Mom, Dad and Laura in the waiting room surrounded by anxious people and bad TV. We took turns holding Allena, needing her physical reminder that life still goes on. She was a miracle; I prayed that we might experience another. We were told Mark might not be able to see, talk or walk again given the location and long-reaching tentacles of the tumor. If, that is, he made it through surgery at all.

At about hour five, I began rising to my feet every time I saw a gurney wheeled from the operating room to intensive care. At hour six, I saw him, his distinct Wyatt Earp mustache giving him away. He saw me too. "Oh, hi Beth," he said nonchalantly, as if we were passing each other in the hallway of our home. Everyone rushed out, unable to believe that Mark was not only living but awake, seeing, talking, moving, able to recognize us and in typical good humor.

"We got it all," the surgeon informed us, referring to the cancerous tumor.

It was a miracle.

Mark was released two days later. The brain swelling that occurs after surgery created all kinds of interesting behaviors in him. Walking around the block, we couldn't make it ten feet before he would grab my hand, point to some moonlit plant and say, "Look, Beth! Can you believe how beautiful it all is, alive with the presence of God?" There was something he no longer feared after surgery, a deep darkness was no longer present in his body or spirit. For the first time he experienced what he had sought all his life: he *felt* the presence of God.

Mark was returning to us, more whole then ever before. His boys, four, seven and nineteen, would continue to have a father. After two terrifying weeks, though we knew there would be other difficulties in the journey, the main challenge was over. I began to breathe again.

THE UNACCEPTABLE

Twelve days after the miracle surgery, Mark's brain herniated while he was sitting in the emergency room. Laura had taken him in after his headaches would not subside. No one realized what was happening until it was too late. A hole was drilled in his head to release the pressure of the fluid that was pushing his brain down into his brain stem. He was put in a medical-induced coma for a week to give him rest from the extreme brain damage that had occurred. Family and friends began a twenty-four-hour bedside vigil, watching, praying, hoping for a miracle.

I sat next to Mark's body wondering how much of Mark was still present. I stared in disbelief at the machines breathing for him, feeding him, keeping him "rested"; tubes in his throat, nose, arm and side. I couldn't pray. I could only stare in silence.

I closed my eyes and pictured Mark riding on the spare tire bolted to the back of his Suzuki Samurai through the Baja desert as I drove. Hot desert air blowing against his happy face thoroughly enjoying the 360-degree view of the stark landscape with Aretha Franklin blaring from the cheap speakers. I had taken a photograph in that moment, impressed by my ability to drive and shoot. Mark looked completely elated, like a dog with its head out the window of a speeding car, his hair sticking straight up in the wind.

I opened my eyes to see Mark lying motionless.

I closed them quickly.

No, this can't be. I then went to the memory of Mark and me riding on the front of a train barreling through Copper Canyon, deep in the Mexican interior. Mark had heard that sometimes the engineer would allow people to stand at the very front of the engine on a little walkway behind a tiny metal bar. I saw his face smiling at me, his pleasure racing through beauty, the thrill, the wind, the wild adventure.

Memories kept coming, all in stark contrast to the reality that lay a few feet away. This time I have just crested a hill on my bike and am starting the long downhill stretch on our pilgrimage in Spain. I grip my brakes and begin to gingerly make my way down the mountain pass when Mark comes screaming up from behind. "Let go, Beth! Let go. Let the hill take you. It's great—come on!"

I felt so much confusion. I believed God was active in orchestrating Mark's amazing journey through surgery, but if so, did that mean God was absent when his brain was herniating? This part of the journey seemed so unnecessary, such a mistake, so completely preventable. Something of my faith—that childlike, magical thinking that God can kiss our hurts and make them go away—was left behind in the ICU, left there with the parts of my brother that never came back from that cold, sterile room filled with beeps and tubes and flashing numbers.

"I need you, Mark," I pleaded. "I need you to tell me it will be okay, to not worry about tomorrow, to find the beauty. I need to hear you say, 'Let go, Beth. You can do it. All will be well.'"

He wasn't able to speak these words to me then. What unfolded was a journey of losing my brother in different ways over the next five years of his life. I could not sing Mark's favorite verse of Leonard Cohen's "Hallelujah": "And even though it all went wrong, I'll stand before the Lord of Song with nothing on my lips but Hallelujah." I had no idea how to accept the unacceptable. Mark would know.

PRAYER PRACTICE: *Breath Prayer*

At times we are unable to pray in any sort of typical way. We just need to catch our breath. These are good times for breath prayer.

The most well-known breath prayer is called the Jesus Prayer, and is "Lord Jesus Christ, have mercy on me." It has been lengthened to "Lord Jesus Christ, Son of God, have mercy on me, a sinner." The prayer is prayed by thinking or saying "Lord Jesus Christ" on the inhale and "have mercy on me" on the exhale. This prayer comes from Luke 18 and is presented beautifully in the spiritual classic and a favorite book of mine, *The Way of the Pilgrim*, written anonymously by a Russian monk. A breath prayer is repeatedly spoken on the lips with the rhythm of our breaths, then slowly drops down from our minds into our bodies where it connects with the very beating of our hearts.

Listen to the yearnings in your heart.

Allow God to call you by name.

Then ask God, "What do I want or need right now?" It might be peace, strength, hope or to know that God is present.

Engage by connecting these needs to the most comfortable way you have of speaking about God: Saving One, Gracious Lord, Holy Spirit, Emmanuel, Abba or Amma, Jesus. A breath prayer is usually not more than eight syllables, said easily with the breath.

Connect with God by praying out your breath prayer, allowing God to adjust and deepen this intimate prayer over the next days.

Try praying your prayer with every breath for five minutes a day, then increase as you desire or when you're feeling anxious or fearful or when you can't sleep at night.

"Abba, I belong to you" is an example of a breath prayer used by Brennan Manning. Other examples include: "Lord, save me," "You, O Lord, are my strength and shield," and "O come, O come, Emmanuel."

seven

Losing My Religion

LORD, you have seen this; do not be silent.
Do not be far from me, Lord.

PSALM 35:22 (NIV)

I USED TO THINK THE strong and silent type was sexy. I also used to think that if I was trapped in a free-falling elevator and jumped at just the right second I wouldn't get hurt. Beliefs change, and so do preferences. I now find the strong and silent type unappealing, particularly when it's God. I prefer the God who says things like "As a mother comforts her child, so I will comfort you" (Isaiah 66:13), and who is quick to assure me that this bruised reed will not be broken (Isaiah 42:3; Matthew 12:20). If I were to write the script, that would be the God who would have come swinging down to rescue me from the dark, confusing jungle of brain cancer, brain injury, hospice and having to say goodbye to a brother long before I was ready.

Many of my prayers during those dark days, if I was able to utter them at all, started something like this: "God, are you kidding me?" Of course, they didn't always start that way. When this dark pilgrimage began, my prayers sounded more like a child's desperate pleas: "Please, please, please, God . . . heal, help, come, rescue!" Then they slowly moved into cries for guidance: "What should we do?" "How can we care for him?" "Where will the money come from?" "Please, show us the way." The silence that followed was deafening.

To quote C. S. Lewis in *A Grief Observed*, it was as if God had slammed the door, and I could hear "a sound of bolting and double bolting on the inside." I tried desperately to hear something, even the clearing of a throat so I'd know someone was there. But when prayer after prayer went unanswered and no throat clearing was to be heard, I eventually stopped asking.

WHEN GOD IS SILENT

Ever since my youth, I have felt God's presence in a loving, intimate way. In this dark time, I listened to the silence, hoping I'd get a "Hey!" every now and then. And I wondered why God had chosen to remain silent. Sometimes I felt like the wallflower at a middle school dance, trying to look like she didn't care but desperately hoping to be noticed.

I had no idea that my pilgrimage of faith would involve losing my religion. At least, that's what it felt like. Much of what I believed about God and the world was not holding up. When this journey of unbelief began, I was deeply shaken. What does one do when they discover God is not who they thought God was? I was birthed into the faith in a pastor's home and raised by a wonderful church community. I wandered around a bit, dipping my toe into various philosophies and world religions before succumbing to my longstanding love affair with Jesus. Since then I had put myself through seminary and entered into a life of ministry. To paraphrase what Peter so beautifully and hopelessly says in John 6:68, "Where else would I go?"

Scarcity became a new reality and unwelcome bedfellow that chased the childlike belief in God's protection and provision right out the door. I felt the scarcity of financial resources as we struggled to figure out how to care for Mark's increasing needs. I felt the scarcity of wisdom as we struggled to make decision after decision for Mark's care and treatment. Where was the guidance? I had always believed that where the Spirit of God is, there is abundance. If we seek God's guidance, God will give us what we need to make it through difficult times. "Way will open," I believed, to use the old Quaker expression.

Sometimes "way opens" way too slowly. Sometimes we do not have what we need. Some seasons we are not able to find the abundance that flows mysteriously under the surface of things. Some days just need to go by. "Lord, please help me go to sleep and wake up in a different part of my story," I journaled.

I was not, of course, allowed to "go to sleep." Instead I watched this slow-motion tragedy unfold before my eyes day after day after day until finally, and forty years too soon, Mark took his last breath and was gone. Removed from the rest of our lives.

Pilgrimage

I was a reluctant pilgrim on this dark journey of terminal illness, more reluctant than my brother, it seemed. Mark would live for five more years after he had the herniation in the emergency room. He spent seven days in the medically induced coma before coming back yet again to us. During those five years he would say things like, "Beth, I have no regrets," and "We'll just play it where it lays," using a golfing metaphor.

Eight years prior to Mark's brain cancer diagnosis, the two of us, along with our spouses and friend Bobby, embarked on a much more joyous pilgrimage, and one of our own choosing. We bicycled five hundred miles across Northern Spain in the pilgrimage of Santiago de Compostela (Saint James). Yellow arrows pointed the way of the ancient pilgrimage route, which at times wove through vineyards, down cobbled streets, past crumbling abbeys, skirting cow pastures, and occasionally joining crowded highways. "Stay on the way!" we'd yell to each other as encouragement, "Stay on the Camino!"

Sometimes I'd purposely steer off the path into a side street just to hear my brother yell, "Stay on the way!" Or I'd pretend to have given up and veer into the middle of an open field, as Mark yelled in feigned hysteria, "Beth, stay on the way! Stay on the Camino!"

So, how do we "stay on the way" when we experience periods of prolonged silence from God, when we are forced to figure out which of the "promises of God" are true and which ones are wishful thinking, rooted more in a need for security than in the mysterious otherness of God? These are the questions I wrestled with. I figured I had two choices. I could either give up on God altogether, since the one I thought I knew seemed to have left the building, or I could wait. And if I waited long enough, maybe God would reveal God's self to me in a new way.

This was a spiritual crisis to be sure. A forest fire had blazed through the landscape of my faith, leaving ashes and singed remnants of a once vibrant Christianity. I needed the help of listening and compassionate friends, the faith and prayers of others, and stories of those who had also suffered and not just survived but whose devastating experiences eventually pushed them into places of growth and beauty. I needed these people to sit with me in the ashes a la Job's friends. But instead of telling me why God was doing this or what I should do, as Job's friends continuously tried to do, I needed them to sit quietly and maybe point out the tiny buds of life pushing through the burnt soil.

What was beginning to surface in me was a hidden belief that if I do certain things, God will reward me in certain ways. When this didn't happen, I was left with deep disappointment. I've worked hard, made sacrifices, tried to do things right, and God has let me down. I don't actually believe this theologically, that my acting dictates God's behaviors in such a direct one-plus-two-equals-three manner, but I was unconsciously operating under this belief.

As I read the psalms, I discovered that my journey of childlike belief and the loss of some of that belief is not a journey of moving away from God but part of *the* journey all of us are on who seek to honestly engage with God throughout a lifetime. The laments are the prayers offered after the chair has been pulled out from under the people of God. They are the "Where are you, God?" psalms. They are the "Why aren't you protecting and providing for us?" psalms. They are, as Walter Brueggemann so helpfully puts it, the Psalms of Disorientation. Aren't we God's chosen people? Didn't God say he would protect us, and lead us through the wilderness, and care for our every need? Their expectations about God, themselves and the world have been shattered, their understandings of God forever altered.

The Psalms of Lament teach me how to pray in the dark. They help me see that God is bigger than both my current felt experience of God and my past assumptions. There is ample room for doubt, anger and confusion in our journey of faith. Reading the psalms might even lead me to believe that if I don't come up against some serious loss of faith from time to time, I might be carrying around a very small God.

This seems to be the pattern: We think we know who God is and who we are in relation to God, our understandings are shattered through some experience, God comes along and eventually gives us a new and greater understanding of God, and just when we think we've got it figured out, the cycle repeats. The mystics call this illumination, purgation and union. I call it painful, unless, as many saints believed, this cycle is more of an upward spiral than a merry-go-round, leading us "further up and further in."

It's hard to see the big picture when you're fumbling around in the dark trying to find the chair that's no longer underneath you. So I follow the prayer template the laments give me and pour my raw emotions out to God.

This I can do.

The Psalms of Lament give me the instructions I need to keep me honest and connected with God in the silence. The Psalms are, after all, the prayer book that Jesus used in his pilgrimage on earth, crying out in his time of greatest need, "My God, my God, why have you forsaken me?" (Psalm 22:1; Matthew 27:46).

"God, are you kidding me?" is a pretty good opening to a lament it seems to me, and in this way, I am staying on the way.

Yes, dear brother, I will stay on the Camino.

PRAYER PRACTICE: *Writing a Lament*

Review some of the Psalms of Lament, such as Psalm 10; 13; 22; 35; 43; 44; 89; 102.

Listen to a loss that is inside of you wanting some acknowledgment.

Write some words that come to mind when you're thinking about this loss. Let them flow free-association style. Try not to edit or judge what comes to mind.

Engage and connect. Write your psalm by using the following template:

1. Address your prayer to God by writing down a name you use for God.

2. The complaint: Pour out your honest, raw emotions to God (even "inappropriate" rage—for example, "Dash their babies against the rocks"—if desired). You are letting God know exactly how you feel.

3. The petition: Ask God to act decisively. Tell God exactly what you want God to do. This is often spoken as a bold imperative. "Awake," "Answer me," "Save me," "Help me," "Come." There are no "pretty pleases" here.

4. Remember how God has been with you in the past. Write about a time or place where you felt particularly close to and loved by God.

The next step is to be written and prayed at some future time, when God has revealed God's self. Do not rush into step five. Try as we might, we do not get to control when this will happen.

5. Praise: This part consists of an assurance of having been heard and the gratitude and praise that naturally flows from the healing, restorative, transforming work that the Lord has done. The God who has seemed absent is now recognized as generous and faithful and saving.

- eight -

Falling into Depression

If you're going through hell, keep going.

WINSTON CHURCHILL

IT WAS ALWAYS MARK who tended toward depression, never me. He was the philosophical one, the brooding artist and intellectual. Mark's first word was *megadoosh* (I kid you not). Mine was *ba*, which Mom and Dad generously interpreted to mean "ball." At times, Mark could be full of hope and clarity, but he was also prone to seasons of sadness. As a child, I was happy and unquestioning. Children are allowed to think in black and white, and that was something that suited my personality well. Mark came out of the chute thinking in shades of gray, no doubt a product of his high IQ.

Darkness came creeping into my spirit as I watched Mark during the last five years of his life. He had come back to us after his brain herniated, but it was hardly a "happily ever after." The person I knew was deteriorating before our eyes because of the cancer and the brain injury that resulted from the herniation. It made sense to me that I'd be depressed. "How could I *not* be affected in this way?" I thought.

What caught me off guard, however, was the dark channel that opened surrounding other parts of my life. My paradigm of marriage was crumbling, and I was thrown by my inability to find sufficient spiritual and emotional resources to get me through. I was deeply unhappy.

TRYING TO BECOME DENMARK

In studies of the happiest countries in the world, the Danes come out on top. Why? Some findings point to their low expectations. I am painfully aware that so often it is my high expectations that get me into trouble. My high expectations are dispersed generously on God, myself, my spouse and the world in general. The thing is, no one—not even God!—seems to be able to live up to them. The problem, of course, is that one cannot simply say to oneself, "Stop having high expectations." Believe me, this does not work; expectations are hard to let go.

Yet lowering expectations is needed, as Donald Miller proclaims in *A Million Miles in a Thousand Years*. "When you stop expecting people to be perfect, you can like them for who they are," Miller writes. "And when you stop expecting God to end all your troubles, you'd be surprised how much you like spending time with God."

Yes, I desperately wanted God to end my troubles and Joe to solve the problems of the intense emotional pain I was experiencing. What I did *not* know was how to dismantle the expectations that were thoroughly ingrained in my DNA.

In the end, I learned that intense and prolonged suffering does the trick.

HITTING BOTTOM

I'm not sure the exact day my spirits hit bottom.

Since Mark's brain herniated, his brain was causing a slow-motion train wreck in his life and those who loved him.

He was released from the hospital to a rehab hospital where he spent the next many weeks. When he finally came home, he was not the same. He was at times impulsive, irrational, lacking inhibition and unable to understand or respond to the needs of others.

Add to that my husband and me losing our jobs and business during a time of recession, leading to intense marital stress, and two toddlers that needed constant attention and energy I didn't have to give. I found myself groping and groveling along what I could only hope was "bottom." When there, of course, one has no idea whether things will get worse; things can *always* get worse. I also did not know how long one could be at the bottom. Doesn't one hit bottom and then come up again? I groped my way along a dark and claustrophobic place for far longer than I thought possible, but the day I knew for sure I had landed in the deepest depths was the day when I

- withdrew all our remaining savings to cover our rent (with no jobs on the horizon, no more money to drain);

- went through my address book and tried to figure out how to separate from Joe; and

- called my doctor to get a prescription for antidepressants.

"All hope is gone," I wrote in my journal. "It's no use pretending anymore."

This was a time of gaining expertise in areas I never wanted to be an expert in. I sat in bankruptcy court holding our new baby, watching my husband go up before the judge, acknowledging publicly our failure. I sat in doctors' offices with my brother learning about brain cancer. I sat with Mark and Laura in the emergency room while his brain was herniating. I then sat in seminars learning how to be a caregiver to someone who has brain damage. I sat with Laura in intensive care on three occasions after Mark had been beaten up due to his new impulsive, brain-impaired behavior. I sat in the county jail waiting for Mark to be released after yet another such incident.

I spent time standing too. I stood in line for food stamps and in the social service office applying for medical assistance. I stood in line to apply for services for which we were eligible, unable to decipher them despite my two master's degrees.

I used to laugh at one of Mark's favorite T-shirts, quoting Shakespeare: "Kill all the lawyers" it read, based on the belief they were just out to make a buck. During that darkest period, Joe and I sat with two kind and effective lawyers, for whom we will always be immensely grateful.

I used to believe government assistance was for lazy and uneducated people who couldn't get their lives together. Suddenly, "they" looked a lot like me.

My slow and subtle descent into depression took four years. I believe it started the day Mark's brain herniated, when it became obvious that things were never going to be the same again. I didn't call it depression or recognize it as such at the time. The antidepressants did not take me out of the claustrophobic place I found myself in, so, I reasoned, I must not be depressed. But the world was dark, even with two of the most preciously intoxicating human beings toddling under my nose.

DISCOVERING THE U-BEND

I hated who I was becoming in this dark season, especially around my kids. There were moments when I felt a rage that I could not control. There were moments I felt unsafe around my own children. I realized that I could physically hurt them, something I had never believed I was capable of. Throughout my twenties, I worked with abused children and was disgusted by the "monsters" who could harm innocent children. Could "they" be me?

I felt the scarcity of emotional and mental resources as my margins of sanity narrowed and rage rushed into the tight places. Some days I couldn't recognize who was looking back at me in the mirror, new stress lines appearing under dimming blue eyes. I was doing all the things I could think of to deal with my stress. I surfed. I sat in my favorite coffee houses. I went to church. I tried to connect deeply with friends. I kept appointments with my spiritual director. I drank wine. I prayed.

None of it was enough.

One day I wandered to the neighborhood coffee house where I sank down in the corner, staring off into space, depleted, unable to focus, my backpack full of bills to pay. As I sat and tried to catch my breath, my eyes wandered to the stack of magazines. *The Economist* sat on top, a magazine I rarely peruse. This day it became manna from heaven. The cover read: "The Joy of Growing Old (or Why Life Begins at 46)." I picked it up and flipped to the article inside: "Age and Happiness: The U-bend of Life."

The article looked at a new branch of economics that seeks to measure human well-being beyond the standard money-based measurements. The researchers discovered that life is not a long slow decline in happiness from birth to death but rather a "U-bend." This means most of us start life happy, at the top of the "U" (like I was in my idyllic hometown as a girl, with the go-karts and sense of the divine), then drop down into unhappy places in the middle of our lives, then come up again in our older years.

I had begun to unpack my bags in the unhappy land of scarcity and relentless anxiety, believing that my depressed spirit and depleted energy was going to continue downward over the course of the rest of my life. But this article was telling me that people are the least happy in their forties and early fifties and become *more* happy and content with life as they grow older! Forty years of data taken from seventy-two countries shows that "although as people move towards old age they lose things they treasure—vitality, mental sharpness and looks—they also gain what people spend their lives pursuing: happiness." In these words, the Holy Spirit took my downcast eyes and directed them outward, toward a horizon filled with hope.

Who would have thought *The Economist* was holy writ?

This article appeared at exactly the right moment, as did Richard Rohr's book *Falling Upward,* in which he describes the necessary shattering of our security structures in moving us into our deeper selves. And Anne Lamott always seems to find her way into my dark places, this time saying to me in *Stitches,* "Unfortunately, forward thrust turns out not to be helpful in the search for your true place on earth. But crashing and burning can help a lot. So, too, can just plain running out of gas."

These voices, from a reporter for *The Economist,* a Catholic theologian and a sacredly irreverent author, told me that the deadness I was feeling was not the end of the story but only the middle. I was experiencing necessary loss in my divinely led journey toward wholeness and home.

This is not to say *specific* loss is necessary for growth. God did not sow cancer cells in my brother's brain so that I might be a happier, more compassionate person. No. But what we are left with when things go wrong—the shattered expectations, the failures, the things we can't control or figure out, the breaking open of our hearts—are necessary and used by God to move us beyond our ego-driven limitations.

Maybe even the depression that filled my spirit was somehow part of this mysterious journey.

Maybe God was there too, in all things working for the good of those who love him, as Romans 8 assures us.

The Economist article ends by explaining that the consequences of this U-bend go beyond emotional well-being. As our stress levels decrease and happiness increases, our wounds heal twice as fast. Hmm, maybe kisses can magically heal once again.

I realized that I had hit the bottom of the U-bend. A little hope crept into my spirit. "They say the darkest hour is right before the dawn," Bob Dylan sings. *Please*, I prayed, let it be so.

PRAYER PRACTICE: *Prayer Postures*

In the throes of grief or exhaustion or depression, we often are not able to engage in mental and verbal prayers. This is a good time to allow our bodies to express our needs to God through prayer postures.

Scripture shows us that people have allowed their body positions to be expressions of prayer for thousands of years. It wasn't until I tried some myself that I began to understand why. Something powerful takes place when our bodies express the truths of our experiences.

Sometimes I stand tall, arms up high, evoking feelings of strength and praise or expectancy, like a child waiting to be picked up by a parent. Sometimes my hands are open, inducing release or requests of help. Sometimes I kneel, recognizing need or contrition. Sometimes I lay on the ground tucked into a fetal position, in fear and need of protection and comfort. Sometimes I lay on my back with arms open wide, evoking prayers of openness, vulnerability and acceptance. Other times I lie prostrate, face down in submission, humility and repentance. I also find myself bowing my head in reverence, placing my hand over my heart or stomach or head to receive God's healing touch or blessing and making the sign of the cross, marking myself as belonging to Christ.

Listen. Ask yourself, *What position does my body want to take right now?* You might try a couple of postures to see what feels the most true.

Engage and connect by simply holding the posture for as long as you desire, allowing your body to offer this wordless prayer.

part two

LISTENING TO
OUR LOSSES

nine

Minimizing Our Wounds

It's just a flesh wound.

THE BLACK KNIGHT,
in *Monty Python and the Holy Grail*

THERE ARE PLENTY OF good reasons to deny or minimize our loss. Grieving, after all, is painful, takes energy and can open us to other unaddressed losses. Grief forces us to admit to our human vulnerability, that we are not in control of the things that matter most to us. This is downright terrifying.

The problem is, our hearts are meant to be listened to. When our hearts are broken and we try to cover over the complicated feelings, bad things happen. We each respond to these "bad things" uniquely. I become irritable. I begin to blame those closest to me (namely my husband, Joe) for not making my world a safer place. I decide an extra glass of wine is not only needed but deserved, and I end up numbing out by way of some screen that connects me to the "world" so I don't have to connect to my heart. I drift slowly away from everything I love.

I find myself thinking, *If my beliefs don't give me a way to accept and deal honestly with all that life brings, then why not hop on*

whatever pleasure train I feel like hopping on? With the accumu-
lation of little things that I don't even name or acknowledge, I bleed
out slowly, and sometimes not so slowly, like in the humorously
graphic scene in *Monty Python and the Holy Grail*. The knight in-
sists, "It's just a flesh wound," while his severed arms lie by his side.

I lose my life blood while insisting I've only got a scratch.

A GRIEF IGNORED

I practiced ignoring grief after a surfing injury sentenced me to
three months in a recliner a few years before our children were
born. While being forced to sit and do nothing is a fate some people
might only dream of, it sent me sinking into despair, questioning
my worth as a human being. The physical damage had come when
my ribs collided with the thin edge of my surfboard after a perfectly
consistent wave had unexpectedly closed out. For days I sat, sipping
tiny breaths, afraid to sneeze for fear of pain, unable to do anything
productive. I became more and more irritable with Joe, who did
nothing but help me with an absurd amount of patience and
kindness. I couldn't stand the feeling of helplessness.

One night as I sat awake and alone in our San Diego loft, tortur-
ously confined to my soft leather chair, I began to verbalize something lurking underneath my cracked ribcage. It started with the
obvious, "I can't move; I can't breathe deeply," then continued, "I
can't clean up this messy house, I can't even pick up after myself, I
. . . can't . . . feel . . . useful . . . I . . . can't . . . even . . . have . . . a . . .
baby." Staying busy had kept me from having to feel the pain of the
confusing fertility journey I was on at the time.

It was then that I noticed the homeless man keeping watch with
me from the alcove across the street. For the next two months he
slept in the doorway as I attempted to sleep three stories up in my
soft recliner. Somehow his presence served as a sentinel and gave
me courage. He was there every night in the cold and darkness. He,

and the dozens of other homeless men and women living in my neighborhood, did not have the luxury of going inside a warm building and sleeping in comfort. His presence helped me choose to not tuck inside a false construct of comfort by denying the painful reality I was experiencing. With the help of his constant nightly presence, I began to have a conversation with God in the midst of what felt like a cold, dark place of not being able to conceive a child. Although I never had the opportunity to meet him, my work with my church's homeless outreach became a way of saying thanks.

When I was able to acknowledge honestly my need, I awakened to God's presence in this dark place. It was easier not to face the confusion and fear lurking deep within, but it was not better. The disconnect was keeping me from myself, from God and from those I loved. The homeless angel came to say what angels always come to say: "Do not be afraid. God is here in this dark place." The nightly conversation with God that unfolded turned one of the most confining experiences into a time of intimacy that still fills me with a sweet longing, a divine kiss that lingers in my memory.

Minimizing Loss

In my work as a spiritual director, I often meet with people who minimize their experiences of loss. In almost everyone's story, disappointments are present. Sometimes they are openly acknowledged. Sometimes they are shyly hidden and in need of a safe place to come out. Sometimes they are forcefully held at bay.

The intention in spiritual direction is to help a person notice God's presence more deeply in their life and circumstances. Often people express a frustration, usually self-directed, such as, "I'm not praying like I should," and slowly a loss emerges. "My mom died this year." "My spouse is not as supportive as I thought she would be." "A terrible thing happened to a friend of mine." "I'm overwhelmed by my new job." Apparently in our society, and in our minds, we are not allowed to feel these things because there are people starving in Africa, as if each of us is only allotted a small amount of grief and we had better put it to good use on something really important.

I help others do what I am learning to do—to listen to the losses within so that these wounds might be tended to by the One who heals and transforms loss. Where are the poor, the blind, the imprisoned, the leprous places inside my own mind, heart, soul and body? This is what I listen for when meeting with another in spiritual direction because this is where we will find Jesus. We will also find him in places of joy and celebration, no doubt. But I am convinced, through my readings of both the Hebrew Scriptures and the New Testament, that God is especially fond of hurting, marginalized, alienated people and of the broken places within every one of us.

My parents tried to show me early on how to listen to my losses and acknowledge the broken, hurting places inside, but I didn't know how important this lesson was when I was a young child.

BEDTIME PRAYERS

"Dear Lord, please be with Tippy, Pepper, Charlie, Benny, Spunky, Albi and the Fish," the names of my pets spoken in one breath as I lay safely tucked under my covers, Mom kneeling by my side. The names changed through loss and gain. Yet this, my nightly prayer offered for the protection of my menagerie, was spoken throughout all of my childhood years.

My animals were my life. The cages, aquariums and hamster habitrail, with its yellow tubing winding snakelike through large sections of my tiny bedroom, were sure to be the talk of the domesticated animal kingdom. I developed a "free-range" philosophy quite early on, priding myself in giving the various creatures in my care ample space to swim, crawl or scamper. My turtle T. J. got a kiddie pool instead of an aquarium. My rabbit Benny hopped around a section of the backyard instead of a cage. The forty-gallon tank for my three tiny tetra fish might have been a bit extreme, but they were worth it! I remember the sadness I felt at the passing of each of my pets. When I was a child, it seemed obvious to me that living things should not die. Things we love should not have to go away.

When I was six, I discovered my beloved cat and first pet, Pepper, lying dead under the bush outside my bedroom window. I sat heartbroken on my bed, lost, not knowing what to do. I tried to pretend I hadn't found her, believing that somehow this would make it not be true. Eventually I told my mom, who dropped what she was doing and sat beside me.

"It's okay to be sad," she said.

Within minutes Dad appeared out of nowhere. This was odd, as Dad was never home in the daytime. He greeted me with a warm embrace, then disappeared. A few minutes later, and now donning dirtied work clothes instead of suit and tie, he told me to follow him outside. I watched as he tenderly lifted Pepper's lifeless body and carried her to the newly dug grave carefully chosen under the flowering bougainvillea. He then asked me to pick out the headstone from a pile of rocks and write "Pepper" in my own wobbly script. Together we placed Pepper into the ground, tucking her into the earth with soft dirt and flower petals.

Mom and Mark joined us as Dad spoke a few words of comfort and closure. It was nice to have a father who was also the pastor of our congregation give the eulogy at these impromptu funeral services in our backyard. Mostly though, I liked how Dad would just show up, be present and masterfully take care of the situation.

My dad was a busy man and a man whose occupational choice led him to bury numerous people, many under heartbreaking circumstances. Dad was well acquainted with the harsh realities of life. By leaving the church office that day after receiving Mom's call and letting the endless meetings and agendas wait, he honored his little girl's broken heart. Without using many words, I learned from my dad that ones we love sometimes die and that death is a part of life—a hard, sad and difficult part to be sure but a part of life to be accepted like all the rest.

We grieve because life hurts us sometimes.

We also grieve in order to see the beauty, feel the joy, hear the laughter and be touched by God's innumerable graces that course through our veins and sneak into our circumstances.

Through the seeds my mom and dad planted and the losses acquired in the decades since, I am beginning to say, along with Thomas Merton, "Save me from my own, private, poisonous urge to change everything. . . . Then the light of Your joy will warm my life." I am beginning to say yes to God in all that life brings. I am beginning to recognize grief not as an interruption but as a means of transformation and grace. I am beginning to understand that "what is in the way is the way."

PRAYER PRACTICE: *Holding the Tension*

Listen as you reflect on these questions:

- Are there things I tell myself that keep me from acknowledging my losses?

- What have I done in the past when I've experienced loss?

- What has been helpful?

- What hasn't?

- What have I done or been tempted to do that keeps me from acknowledging my loss? (Watch TV? Drink alcohol? Obsessively exercise? Play computer games? Get lost in social media? Work long hours?)

- What losses (big or little) am I able to acknowledge right now?

Many of us don't acknowledge loss because it's painful and creates an uncomfortable tension in us that has no place to go. What we long for is not what we are experiencing. There is a painful disconnect between how things should be and how things are. A spiritual director friend of mine, Maggie, taught me this practice of holding the tension. This is exactly what we need to learn to do—hold, not escape from, the pain.

Engage the tensions you feel by holding your hands out in front of you palms up. Choose one current experience of loss. In your left hand, envision holding the way things should be or the way you want them to be. In your right hand, envision holding the reality that is hurting you at the moment, the ways things currently are. (You may want to write these down and hold the pieces of paper.)

As you allow yourself to feel the discomfort of holding these seemingly opposite things, *connect* with God who is underneath you holding the deeper reality. Transformation does not come by either giving up on what we yearn for or minimizing the painful realities of life but in holding two seemingly opposite things until they are transformed by the loving presence of God. As in all of these practices, feel free to share your experience with another person or small group.

- ten -

Acknowledging Our Losses

Blessed are they that mourn:
for they shall be comforted.

MATTHEW 5:4 (KJV)

WHEN I WAS A CHILD, MOM WOULD swoop me into her arms when life didn't go the way I wanted it to go. She would kiss my hurt places and miraculously make them better. When I was hurt by the actions of another, Mom would pick me up and comfort me by rocking me in the rocking chair as I cried, "It's not fair," until I was exhausted. As my world became more confusing and complicated, I stopped letting Mom comfort my heart and heal my knees. I no longer burst into tears when life hurts me, like I see my children do. And in growing up, I've lost some honesty. Now, my first response to pain is "I'm fine" as I busy myself with important projects, motherly duties and spider solitaire.

"WHY" AND "ALREADY"

Instead of asking "How can I be comforted?" when pain gets too loud to ignore, I ask, often coupled with an expletive or two, "Why did this happen to me?" I cry. I shake my fists. I look for someone to blame.

Why is the most unhelpful word I can't stop saying. I have a long history of crying out, "Why?"

When we were growing up, my brother's bedroom had two windows, and mine only had one. It seemed like Mark never even looked out the window. I sat in my windowsill for hours. I can't count the times when Mom would try to comfort me in the rocking chair as I cried out, "Why?" to some such atrocity that rocked my little world. (It doesn't take much, I know.) And I haven't changed much, but eventually I wear myself out. The whys never seems to get me anywhere. They don't make the situation go away, which is what I'm wanting. "Why?" always disappoints.

Fortunately, I eventually give up on the whys and get to the business of reconnecting with the God who is already present. I begin to ask "what" questions, such as "What can I do in this unwanted situation?" Sooner or later the golden "where" question arises: "God, where are you in this?" Which in turn leads me to "how": "How are you inviting me to be in this?" This often takes time, but it is a way forward in times of loss. These questions remind me that God does the deep work of healing, restoration and rebuilding trust. My job is to try to pay attention.

Amid all my questioning, a little, somewhat uninteresting word tumbled out between the lines of Scripture, bringing the reality of God's presence home. It's not a sexy word or spiritual sounding, yet it's a word that whips my mental distractions into shape, interrupts my theological wanderings, and gives me a focus and clarity that has become a foundation and guide for my life. The word is *already*.

I first noticed its presence in the passage in Mark 4:38 where the disciples are in a storm fearfully watching the winds and waves overtake their little vessel. And where is Jesus? He is already in the boat . . . sleeping—on a cushion!

The point is, I don't pray him into a situation; he is *already* there. That is all I need to remember. When I am overwhelmed, frightened, feeling out of control, unable to handle what life brings, Jesus is already present. Perhaps he is waiting for me to cry to him for help, perhaps he is beckoning me to crawl in next to him and fall asleep on the cushion in the midst of the storm. Whatever the invitation, he is there. So my question has become "What can I do to notice Jesus' presence with me here and now?"

This is why I became a spiritual director. I love to go God-hunting with people and help them notice a whisper or a footprint where they least expect it. I love to sit with people experiencing a full divine embrace and bathe in the beautiful consolations of God. I also love to sit with people in the agony of God's silence because I know that if we sit long enough, we will eventually, to quote Meister Eckhart, hear the God who is "like a person who clears his throat while hiding and so gives himself away." We will hear the invitation and see the One who is already here and has been present with us all along. And as I sit with another on their sacred journey, I am reminded that God is intimately in the midst of my journey too, regardless of my current felt experience, and this helps.

LEARNING TO GRIEVE

Fortunately, in high school, when accumulated losses hit the tipping point, I knew enough to pray. This happened when friends hurt my feelings, when I learned that a trusted Sunday school teacher was having affairs, when people I loved became seriously ill, when some far-away tragedy devastated part of the world. I created an altar in my room at night with a cross and candle. Then I wrote down names of people and situations that were weighing heavy on me and prayed them out to God. This helped.

During the loneliness of college, I began to walk the beach. I'd walk in one direction pouring my confusion out to God until I said all that was in me to say; then I'd turn around. As I walked back I would attempt to listen or just watch wave after wave fold onto the shore and feel the touch of cold, wet sand under my bare feet. This helped.

In my twenties, I spent long hours in coffee houses pouring all the disappointments onto pages of my journal. "Father," I would begin, and then I would pour out my thoughts ending with, "Help! Please." This helped.

In my late twenties, after a long, confusing church experience and deepening cynicism toward men and relationships, I began to frequent a monastery. There, I sat for hours alone in the stark desert wilderness. I sat in the chapel five times a day and listened to the comforting voices of monks chanting the Psalms over me. This helped.

During this same period I was encouraged to attend a retreat by my then ex-boyfriend Joe. I sat disengaged in the corner until I heard the words, "Our deepest places of hope and vision often correspond to our greatest places of wounding." These words pierced me and began to unravel a tight knot inside. My despair and cynicism surrounding relationships with men and the church corresponded to my areas of greatest vision. This helped.

Looking back, I can see many ways I sought comfort amid life's storms. I wouldn't have recognized these to be means of grieving or spiritual practices, but I intuitively knew that the only way to stay open to life was to stay honest and open to what was going on inside of me and to pour it out to God.

GRAY IS NOT MY FAVORITE COLOR

On a recent road trip, I woke up in the freezing predawn hours, threw on my boots and jacket, and left the kids and Joe asleep in our cozy motel room. I was embodying John Muir as I trudged through the bitter cold in a snowstorm to the rim of the Grand Canyon, determined to see the canyon come to life, to watch the sunrise slowly illuminate the canyon walls, a once-in-a-lifetime experience. It didn't dawn on me until I was actually standing behind the guardrail on the precipice that jutted into the canyon that one cannot see anything in a snowstorm—anything but gray.

Later that day, I realized how much this image illustrates my life. Gray is not my favorite color. I yearn to see bright, clear colors, and I'm startled to find that gray is often the reality presented to my senses. I want to see the clarity of consistency, fairness, love, health and happiness, not the muted shades of sickness, disillusionment, confusion, anxiety and despair. But that afternoon, for one precious moment, I was able to stand deeply present in my life of gray and laugh. I laughed that morning as I stood on the edge of the Grand Canyon, laughed at my ridiculous effort to make something happen without regard to obvious external realities. And I laughed that afternoon because I realized the sun was still there, already present, rising. The canyon was waking up, as it does every morning, all around me, underneath me and far beyond. This was the reality. I just couldn't see its unfolding that day.

One of the most essential lessons I've learned about grief is that we do not get to choose what to grieve. It chooses us. Grief turns life gray, and sometimes it takes a while for our eyes to adjust to what's there and to believe there is a deeper reality present underneath. Our job is to listen to our heart and body and acknowledge what is hurting us. Our job is not to decide what wounds are worth grieving or to judge as insufficient whatever is hurting us.

We do not choose what to grieve, but we can choose to grieve what we find.

It's always easier for me to "keep on keepin' on" rather than to deal with the negative emotions I've experienced that turn my internal landscapes into shades of gray. But I'm discovering that "keepin' on" through minimizing, ignoring or disconnecting from the things that hurt me shuts down my heart and keeps me from mourning. My relationships suffer, and I become disconnected from the One who brings comfort.

Here are a few unhelpful messages I've told myself or have heard from others that keep me from acknowledging loss:

- I shouldn't feel bad, So-and-So has it so much worse.

- I need to stay strong for my family.

- Women are too emotional. (Real men don't cry.)

- A stronger person wouldn't be so needy.

- Jesus died a painful death for me on the cross; the least I can do is buck up and not focus on my own pain.

Or how about this: I don't want to be one of *those* types of people. Yes, we know the ones we mean, the ones who seem to thrive on personal crisis and somehow manage to use their sufferings as a weapon of manipulation.

In my experience, very few people need to concern themselves with over-acknowledging or over-reacting to loss. For most of us, the opposite is true. We need to find ways to trust what our body is telling us and acknowledge the places of hurt residing within.

Recently, when I found myself depleted and heart-heavy, unable to pinpoint why, I went to see the movie *Les Misérables* with Anne Hathaway playing Fantine. When Hathaway sang "I Dreamed a Dream," I came completely undone. Some long-neglected place opened up in me and I sat mesmerized, tears flooding down my cheeks.

I shared this with my spiritual director friend Jeannie. "Disappointment, shattered dreams, loss of innocence . . ." I rambled, my mind trying to force words into a wordless place. I hadn't experienced any of the hardships Fantine had gone through, yet her words entered into me with a piercing beauty that bypassed my mental ruts, as beauty often does.

"Do you want to see it again with me?" Jeannie asked, and added, "I can sit next to you and you can hold my hand if you need to." Of course I said yes. Jeannie understood that I did not need to talk about what was going on. I needed to find the font of healing that came through Fantine's song in the comfort and encouragement of Jeannie's presence.

I did not need to ask why. What I needed was to allow my feelings of loss to be acknowledged. With the help of a movie and a friend, and a great, big canyon filled with gray, I found the comfort of a God who was already present.

PRAYER PRACTICE: *Imaginative Prayer*

Jesus invited us to use our imaginations when he said things like "I am the door," "I am the vine and you are the branches," "I am the good shepherd." In imaginative prayer, popularized by Ignatius of Loyola in the sixteenth century, we are invited to use our senses and mental images to enter into a story in Scripture in order to experience God's presence through the passage.

Listen to the story of Jesus in the storm from Mark 4:35-41. Read the passage slowly.

> On that day, when evening had come, he said to them, "Let us go across to the other side." And leaving the crowd behind, they took him with them in the boat, just as he was. Other boats were with him. A great windstorm arose, and the waves beat into the boat, so that the boat was already being swamped. But he was in the stern, asleep on the cushion; and they woke him up and said to him, "Teacher, do you not care that we are perishing?" He woke up and rebuked the wind, and said to the sea, "Peace! Be still!" Then the wind ceased, and there was a

dead calm. He said to them, "Why are you afraid? Have you still no faith?" And they were filled with great awe and said to one another, "Who then is this, that even the wind and the sea obey him?"

Engage in the story by becoming one of the characters or a bystander. Notice what you see, smell, taste, touch and hear unfolding around you.

Connect by interacting in the story. Are you saying or doing anything? Is Jesus saying anything to you? Is Jesus doing anything or inviting you to do anything? Feel free to journal, sketch or share your experience with another person or a small group.

- eleven -

Overcoming Our
Obstacles to Grieving

*It isn't for the moment you are struck that you
need courage, but for that long uphill climb
back to sanity and faith and security.*

ANNE MORROW LINDBERGH

ONE OF THE MANY THINGS my brother Mark taught me
was the art of trespassing. "Try every door" was one of his
favorite mottos.

Trespass, he coached, only for purposes of historic exploration
or pursuit of beauty, and always tread lightly, leaving the place nicer
than you found it. He also taught me his paraphrased version of one
of the censored verses of Woody Guthrie's "This Land Is Your Land,"
which we belted out around Baja campfires, me on guitar, Mark on
percussion playing the various bottles and metal objects in reach:

There was a sign there, that tried to stop me;
On one side it said: Private Property;

But on the other side it didn't say nothing;
That side was made for you and me.

One day, during the quarter that Mark and I were both attending UC Santa Barbara, he suggested we visit the Point Conception Lighthouse. When we arrived and began heading toward the heavily barbed-wire fence posted with a No Trespassing sign, Mark explained that we might need to be a little "discreet." He then helped his little sister through a gap between barbs, like a perfect gentleman.

As we walked, he explained that this was privately owned ranch land. "Don't worry," he said attempting to be reassuring, "the intertidal land is always public, so we can walk along the beach if need be." I suggested we make our way in that direction and few minutes later we were standing atop a hundred-foot cliff watching the water lap at its base. "Hmmm, must be high tide," Mark said.

Within minutes we heard the helicopter.

"Run for cover!" Mark yelled, possibly re-enacting one of his green army-men battles, but run we did, realizing we'd been hiking through sand dunes void of vegetation. We dove beneath two pathetic shrubs.

"Dang! They patrol this ranch by helicopter," he shared, stating the obvious.

I was wearing a florescent yellow biking jacket. Hardly inconspicuous. Why didn't Mark tell me what we would be doing today? I would have worn something sand-dune, chaparral colored.

The helicopter seemed to hover a bit but eventually flew away. Mark hopped up laughing and proceeded to jump with flair off the steep edge of the sand dune. When my irritation about his late-in-the-game disclosures subsided, I joined him. Soon we were both laughing, leaping and rolling down the sand dunes together.

We eventually made it to the Coast Guard's gated land, heavily posted "No Trespassing," hopped those fences and peered over the top of a hill to one of the most beautiful scenes I have ever taken in. The Point Conception Lighthouse sat alone on a stunning shock of land, shining white in the noon sun. We stood still taking in all the colors: red tiled roof surrounded by changing shades of green, wind-whipped grass with the deep blue sea just beyond. Then Mark looked at me and smiled. And I could see "I told you so" and "I'm so glad to be sharing this with you" in that smile.

We ran down the hill elated.

It was then we heard voices. Two men in uniform were coming our way.

This time I shouted, "Head for cover!" but there was again no "cover" to head for. Even Mark can't get himself out of this tight spot, I thought.

"No," Mark said, and before I could stop him, he was introducing himself to the retired rear admiral of the Coast Guard and his assistant, a man who, as it turns out, used to be in charge of all West Coast lighthouses. I came down and sheepishly smiled, trying to somehow look like we didn't realize we had just trespassed multiple times to get here. They were obviously alarmed. "How did you get here?" the rear admiral inquired.

"Oh we just sort of wandered," I said, waiting to be arrested.

Mark then asked the rear admiral if he would give us a tour. I couldn't believe it. Is he not reading the situation? They want to arrest us! He proceeded to tell the rear admiral about our love of lighthouses and threw in enough nerdy facts to convince him that we were there for that reason. I watched the admiral's countenance shift.

"Come on, I've got the keys," he said.

INAPPROPRIATE BEHAVIORS

I'm glad Mark taught me there is more to life then playing by the rules and obeying every sign. Listening to our losses means that sometimes we must hop over a few fences. Listening to our losses also involves recognizing the voices we need to tune out. Those who muster up the courage to grieve, or those who simply are no longer able to hide life's devastations, can find themselves marginalized, hearing messages like, "If you *must* grieve, be private, quick and efficient about it," "Don't make others uncomfortable," and for goodness sake, "Be appropriate."

Grief work is culturally inappropriate behavior.

If we are going to honestly tend to our losses, we might feel like we are going against the tide, running from the numbing illusion that everything is always fine. Many around us are unable or unwilling to grieve, hiding from the things that hurt them, escaping the pain and vulnerability woven into the human experience, choosing the way of avoidance instead of the way of the cross. In doing so, however, they also escape the way of new life that comes after the acute pain subsides and slowly resurrects into something else. A grief-immune culture is worth running away from, and grief-restrictive fences are worth hopping over.

For some of us, "keep up appearances" and "don't disappoint the powers that be" were just above "love thy neighbor as thyself" in the unspoken list of family rules. But as we mature, we realize that many rules are meant to be broken, as they bar the way of growth. Many messages we have received no longer need to be obeyed. Every time we break a cultural, family or personal norm, we should expect disappointment to follow. Learning to accept and live with the disappointment we feel from others or even ourselves is often the difficult pathway to freedom.

In grief work, we need to listen to the deeper voices within and ask, "What is needed?" "What fences or cultural norms need to be trespassed?" "Who might I need to disappoint in order to honestly engage in this loss?" Maybe I need to scream or burst out laughing or take a midnight run or break something or call someone I barely know but think might help. Maybe I need to take a road trip or stay in bed for a very long time or shout words I've never shouted before to God or the universe or cancer or death or to an effigy of the person who has disappointed me time and time again. Maybe I need to ask for help.

Who ever thought that behaving inappropriately, ignoring unhelpful messages or friends and family, and disappointing others could be a means of pursuing health and working creatively with loss? I would argue that they might just be.

We all need an inner Anne Lamott to teach us the importance of sacred irreverence. Mark's wife and I share a favorite quote of hers in response to people jovially saying, "Let go and let God." "Believe me, if I could, I would," she responds, then adds, "and in the meantime I feel like stabbing you in the forehead." This makes us laugh until we are in tears. This is not appropriate, but it is exactly what I need in times of grief. It gives me permission not to listen to the unhelpful, often well-meaning messages we've received such as "let go and let God," which have left us feeling more alone and dismissed.

Of course, we need look no further than Jesus to find a person perfectly willing to buck cultural norms and go against the flow as he takes a whip into the temple and creates a huge mess. He refused to obey the "no whipping or turning over tables" signs clearly posted on the temple walls.

Sometimes the posted signs that need to be disobeyed are internal. These are the ones I have created to protect my heart, the hidden promises I've made long ago to stay tough so I won't get hurt again. When it comes to grief work, I am learning which "Private Property" signs posted around my heart to disregard.

Mark has been my teacher here too. He loved bushwhacking through wild places on our earthly landscape, including spelunking, exploring dark underground caverns. He chose to do this in his internal landscape as well, even when that landscape was messy, tangled, mistake-wrought and depression-darkened. He taught me how to be courageous in exploring both the external places I want to go and the internal places I do not want to go. "Keep exploring," he would tell me, even if the places I was heading toward are behind certain signs that begin "Trespassers W," which according to Piglet in one of Mark's and my favorite stories stands for "Trespassers William" and *not* for "Trespassers Will Be Prosecuted."

I need Mark's help to enter into the wild places of grief work, to listen to the hurt places within. He encourages me to explore the ruins and wreckages with a historian's curiosity, ultimately perhaps finding the dark beauty that lies on the other side of the fences. "You can do it, Beth," I hear him say as he sings over me, and I can almost hear Woody and Jesus joining in:

> There was a sign there, that tried to stop me;
> On one side it said: Private Property;
> But on the other side it didn't say nothing;
> That side was made for you and me.

PRAYER PRACTICE: *The Prayer of the Tantruming Child*

When my daughter was very young, at times she would fly into a full-blown tantrum. I have *no idea* where she got such a temper (insert my parents rolling their eyes here). It looked something like this: loud screams and cries with an occasional "I hate you, Mommy" thrown in, followed by mad flailing in my direction. I would move toward her, grab her flailing arms and pull her onto my lap. I'd ask her, "What's the matter?" Sometimes she could tell me, sometimes she could only yell and scream and say mean things.

Eventually she would wear herself out. And if I was lucky, she would collapse into my arms exhausted and fall fast asleep, lulled by the sound of my heartbeat, safe in my arms.

I knew she did not hate me. Her favorite toy had been broken and her little world had fallen apart. I am really no different.

Listen to your hurt and anger and disappointment. Find a safe place (probably not in front of your boss or kids).

Engage in a full-blown tantrum if you can. Go ahead; give all you've got to God. God can take it; just read a few of the psalms and you will see. Yell, flail, cry, say disparaging things, and say them directly to God if disappointment in God is part of your pain. Say them until you have worn yourself out. You might blare music in your car or shower and scream until you are hoarse and exhausted. Hit a pillow, tear apart an old phonebook or break a set of dishes. Remember, "nice" is not a Christian virtue, no matter what our mothers or Sunday school teachers tried to teach us. So go ahead, tantrum. It might be just what is needed to find your way home.

Connect with the One who longs to hold you close. Nothing compares to the dead weight of a sleeping child in your arms. I think God feels this too.

- twelve -

Revealing Our Perspectives

You may be an undigested bit of beef,
a blot of mustard, a crumb of cheese, a fragment
of underdone potato. There's more of gravy than
of grave about you, whatever you are!

CHARLES DICKENS

NIMALS!" MY FRIEND YELLED as she madly began paddling toward shore.

Even with this rather odd description of what she'd seen, I knew
from the tone in her voice and panic in her eyes she had not seen
just any animal. She had seen the one "animal" we hope never to
see up close in the waves—a shark. And not just any shark; there
are plenty of "friendlies" out there sharing our coastal waters, but
she had no doubt seen the dreaded Great White. This shark, thanks
to the movie *Jaws*, has kept so many in my generation out of the
water for good. They are occasionally seen off the California coast
and live up to their bad reputation every few years by brutally
killing a surfer or swimmer.

I whipped around, ready to face my greatest nightmare. With no one else in the water and my friend now paddling toward shore, I knew I could be in trouble. I watched in terror as the large dorsal fin broke the surface. Then the back appeared and before my brain could tell my muscles what to do, up popped the happy smiling head of a dolphin. Sheer panic turned immediately into fits of laughter.

Instead of a frantic paddle to shore I paddled toward this beautiful creature and enjoyed her playful company for a few glorious moments. I slapped the water gently trying to draw her toward me, wanting to touch her smooth skin. She was not as interested, tired of me and swam away. The same event, seen from a different perspective, caused completely different reactions from my friend and me, as different as sheer panic is from fits of laughter. (My friend still gets mad when I tell this story, so I'm not mentioning her name.)

As in this story, sometimes I think I see something clearly, but my perspective is way off. I see danger where there are playful invitations or believe I'm safe and "protected" when in reality I might experience a deep bite or two. Loss has a way of shattering our perceptions. How do we navigate the terrain when our perceptions, beliefs and assumptions don't match the reality unfolding before us?

OUR OPERATING SYSTEM

Part of listening to our losses means becoming aware of our "operating systems," the underlying assumptions that guide our perspectives and help us manage and interpret the world. These assumptions can either help or hinder our healing. My journey to understand that I have a lens, a specific way I view the world, has been a painful, sometimes humiliating, process. I want to believe I see things clearly and am not distorted by my personality, upbringing, family systems and cultural biases. This, of course, is not true. Loss brings my perspectives and assumptions to the surface and has, at times, become a gift of important self-discovery, although a painful one.

Are my current understandings about life, God and the world big enough to hold the experiences I am having? Much of the time my perspectives are unconscious—until they stop working. Loss ushers in the need for a new operating system to explore the ways we view the world, to question what has gone unquestioned, to sift the chaff and seek kernels of truth.

When my husband, Joe, and I were presented with the opportunity to buy a business in downtown San Diego, we approached the idea rationally and prayerfully. A stable income source, we reasoned, could provide Joe with the opportunity to do creative theater work and afford me the ability to continue in my ministry of spiritual direction. When immediate pressure came to make a quick decision, Joe and I knew enough to turn the offer down. We needed more time to research and pray.

After a couple of weeks, however, we discerned that we should go ahead with the idea. Amazingly, the opportunity was still available, so we signed the paperwork and became business owners of a beautiful and successful nature store in a prime location on the San Diego Bay.

This particular story does not end well.

What we believed to be a God-given opportunity ended up taking a deep, destructive bite out of our lives, our confidence, our finances, our future and our marriage. We bought the store during a climate of relative prosperity, unaware of the oncoming recession. Then tourism dropped dramatically and people no longer spent as much money on unnecessary items. We did not have the know-how or the financial resources to weather the storm. All efforts to save the sinking ship that was our only source of income and investment ended in disappointment and bankruptcy. How do I view what happened in light of my belief that God led us into this?

The experience, as it began to unravel, brought to light my under-lying belief that if God leads us into something, that something will be good. Hard, maybe, but destructive? Never!

Where did we go wrong? Were we wrong about our initial dis-cernment? If God led us, how could it not all go well? The questions went deeper: Does God guide our lives? Does God even care about us?

JUDGING OUR EXPERIENCES

One day, when I felt certain my world was falling apart, I shared my woes with a friend. He quipped, rather unsympathetically I thought, "Might not be the end of the world." I was deeply irritated. *Doesn't he understand how awful this is?* I thought.

I am quick to judge my experiences. What feels awful, must be awful, I reason. In this way, I am heartily eating from the tree of the knowledge of good and evil. Taking onto myself a job only suited for God. My spiritual director gently points this out by repeatedly encouraging me through the words of Pierre Teilhard de Chardin. "Trust in the slow work of God." Progress is made, the quote con-tinues, "by passing through some stages of instability." "It might be helpful to try and observe without judgment," she suggests.

Loss shatters. We do not see things clearly, and pieces come back together slowly. But instability and slowness, I am learning, might not always be bad. They might be just what I need to let go of my constant compulsion to judge every moment of my un-folding story. I've come to recognize that refining my operating system and releasing my constant judgments will be a life-long process, as my experiences continue to challenge underlying be-liefs and hidden perspectives.

I remember a verbal game we used to play as children, a deri-vation of a children's book called *Fortunately*. The way we told it on my playground was to begin with the words "There was a boy who fell out of a plane."

"Oh, that's *bad*," the listener would respond.

"There was a haystack below," we'd answer.

"Oh, that's *good*."

"There was a pitchfork in the haystack."

"Oh, that's *bad*."

And on it went with the boy missing the pitchfork (good) and missing the haystack (bad), and so on.

We often don't know how to judge correctly until we get to the *end* of the story.

Grief can be a time of deep questioning, a time when we might realize we were mistaken about the way the world works, about ourselves, and about the nature of our relationships with others and with God. We ask questions in times of loss, questions about how this loss could have happened to me, and real answers, if there are any to be found, tend to be revealed slowly. These things are helpful to know, because it means a little gentleness is needed, a little grace, and wisdom to find the people and resources I need to stay as grounded as possible during difficult times of upheaval.

Sometimes we need to suspend judgment, hold off assumptions and simply let our stories unfold, trusting, as we are able, "in the slow work of God."

PRAYER PRACTICE: *Prayer of Examen*

Road trips in our VW camper van are one of my favorite things ever, and at the same time they can bring out the worst in me. I introduced this prayer practice to my family while on a road trip two summers ago, partly so my kids and husband could express their displeasure about my bad behavior in a constructive way if needed. We have done it every night since.

Ignatius of Loyola recommended that everyone be taught the prayer of examen in order to recognize God's presence and call in the midst of the ordinary stuff of our lives.

Listen to your feelings, moods, thoughts and urgings as you think back over your day. Ask yourself:

- What am I most grateful for today?

- What am I least grateful for?

Other ways to ask these questions include:

- What brought me energy today?

- Where did I feel most connected or loved today, most alive?

- What drained me?

- Where did I feel least loved today?

Engage and connect in this prayer by writing down or sharing with another person where you experienced consolation or gratitude. Then bathe in those feelings, relive the experience and thank God for touching you in this way.

Next, write down or share with another person times when you experienced desolation, discouragement, disconnection or despair. This time, imagine holding the feelings and situation in your hands, not bathing in it or trying to fix or solve it. Simply ask, "God, is there anything for me to notice here?" God can use these things to bring awareness that leads to more life. Then release them to God's care as best you can.

Over time you might notice patterns appear. This can help you discern what to do more of and what to do less of in order to live more fully into the life God has for you.

This prayer practice also reminds us that God is present in both the moments and situations we label as "good" (consolation) and what we often label as "bad" (desolation). This prayer has changed my perspective on many desolations, as some have proved to be a powerful means of awareness and grace.

- thirteen -

Fear of Falling

Ashes! Ashes! We all fall down.

CHILDREN'S NURSERY RHYME

MARK NEVER FELL. He loved to tell the story of a mountain-climbing adventure in Baja. He and his friend Jim decided on climbing Picacho del Diablo (the Devil's Peak) on a whim, without rope or climbing gear. Mark, believing his Converse high tops were as good as any hiking boot or climbing shoe, scaled the last thousand feet or so to the top of the ten-thousand-foot peak.

After descending, he and Jim popped into a bar for a celebratory *cerveza*, where he proudly told the patrons he had just climbed El Picacho *sin ropa*. They looked shocked and impressed, as he hoped they would. It wasn't until later that he realized instead of saying he'd climbed the peak without rope (*sin cuerda*), he had told them he'd climbed the peak without clothes.

Mark was also an avid climber of statues and monuments. Ever since he was a little boy, he'd climb every statue possible, getting shouted down off many by a parent or security guard. Laura accepted this part of her husband and began to photographically document many of his statuary climbs, encouraging him all the more. They made a good team. While Mark and Laura were in Portugal, Mark noticed something and told Laura, "I'll be right back." A few minutes later she began scanning the horizon for Mark and looked up, way up. Mark was sitting fifty feet up in the concrete lap of some great explorer on the towering Monument to the Discoveries.

We have no idea how Mark could climb Spider Man–like straight up metal or concrete all while wearing his black high tops. A slight slip on any number of these could have ended in serious injury or death. But Mark never fell.

Mark never fell, that is, until a few years after his brain injury.

Joe, the kids and I were spending an evening with my brother's family when we heard a loud thump from the hallway. We all ran to find my brother lying on the floor. He had lost his balance and fallen backwards, unable to catch himself. We quickly assessed that he was okay. He didn't even seem too shaken by the event. Laura gathered up her boys to comfort them while Joe and I helped Mark get back on his feet.

I took in everyone's reactions. Mark seemed tired and confused but in relatively good humor. "Why doesn't this body of mine work anymore?" Mark's son who was ten at the time and I both felt panic, his expressed through tears and nervous communication, mine held internally. I acted and reacted coolly but felt a terrifying and overwhelming sadness.

Mark's then seven-year-old seemed unscathed. "I helped Daddy up the other day," he proudly proclaimed. My husband did not seem emotionally affected by the event. I asked Joe in the car ride home if Mark's falling affected him like it did me.

"No," he said. "Mark doesn't have much balance anymore, so falling is part of his life, like a baby's. The good thing is he is still flexible and well padded from his recent weight gain, so he probably won't get hurt when he falls."

LISTENING, NOT JUDGING

This story illustrates an awareness that has been important in my journey of listening to my grief. Like the shark story of the previous chapter, the same event can be experienced in entirely different ways by different people. We all see things from our different perspectives.

I knew this academically, but it wasn't until this experience that I realized we grieve different things for different reasons. So we must not assume or judge ourselves based on others but rather listen to our own hearts. Mark's fall affected me deeply, and that was enough. I didn't need to say, "That's dumb, Beth, he just fell, no biggie." I am learning to listen *without judgment* to what is being revealed in me, so that I might open it to the healing touch of God. Wounds need air to heal, not judgment.

As a spiritual director, I am trained to hold off on assumptive comments like "Oh, that must be painful" or "How great!" until I gather cues from the other person as to the accuracy of these comments for their experience. For example, a Thanksgiving dinner where the whole family gathered might not have been great, it might have been traumatic, and the death of a loved one might have come as a relief instead of a devastation, so I try not to fill in the blanks. Instead, I ask, "How was that for you?" And I listen openly to the response. It's the response I am trained to work with in my ministry: listening deeply to what is there without judgment, looking for Jesus in the midst.

I am trying to translate this into the way I listen to what needs attention in my own life. I am trying to train my own inner voice to ask things like "What is affecting you right now?" instead of the usual dismissive recordings such as "That shouldn't bother you" or "Get over it."

ACKNOWLEDGING FEAR

Mark's fall that evening affected me in another way: I have become afraid of falling. I never feared falling as a kid. Like Mark, I would climb every tree in sight. In college, following Mark's lead, I took up rock climbing and loved climbing a hundred feet or so up sheer rock faces. But now, I no longer have confidence that I won't fall, that all will be well, that certain things won't happen to me or to those I love. The phone ringing late at night no longer means a wrong number; now it means someone I love might have died. When we pack the kids in our old van and head out on a road trip, my brain conjures up images of a tragedy that might be awaiting us on the highway.

When my invincible brother succumbed to cancer, I no longer had the luxury of believing that there are safe places in this world. There is no safe house here, no true sanctuary. Anything can happen to anyone at any time. Most of the time people get up again, but sometimes they do not. And no one is asking for my input on how any of this plays out.

Fear has been a very real part of each loss I have experienced. I am trying to learn how to listen to this fear, acknowledging its presence with tenderness and not judgment. When tragedy strikes, a vulnerable place is opened, a wound received; of course I am afraid. I can see it clearly when watching another suffer, and I am trying to have the same eyes for myself. When we see suffering, compassion is evoked. This compassion has proven vital to my healing.

In the book *Falling Upward*, Richard Rohr speaks of the necessity of falling. "You learn how to recover from falling by falling!" Our falls and failures are what usher us into the second half of life where we are free to live more wholly and fully alive. I am afraid of falling because falling feels out of control. But as I know from surfing, falling is necessary.

When I learned to surf and when I teach people now, there is a natural tendency to ride too far back on the board when paddling for a wave. No one likes to go "over the falls," the term used when the board and rider go plummeting down the face of the wave head-first. The problem is if you hold back, unwilling to go "over the falls" from time to time, you will never catch a wave. Falling is very important in learning how to surf, in finding the perfect position on the board that allows you to dance in the liquid wonderland.

People in all walks of life who are successful in their fields speak of the importance of falling and failing. There is no better learning tool, the website admittingfailure.org recently reminded me. Unfortunately, I think this is true.

Instead of judging my reactions to loss and failure and allowing fear to consume me, I am trying to acknowledge what's there and listen to the judgment and fear. When my children are afraid, I hold them close. In the same way, I am learning that a listening, compassionate presence is what the fearful part of me needs. Fear needs to be listened to and comforted, and wounds need air to heal, not judgment. We all fall down.

PRAYER PRACTICE: *The Stations of the Cross*

In my twenties, I discovered the stations of the cross at a desert monastery. I walked the wilderness path, stopping and praying at the fourteen stations representing Christ's journey toward the cross. As I gazed at the scenes unfolding on painted wood before my eyes, I noticed places inside of me coming to the surface, places of confusion and loss, places where I had "fallen."

Something profound took place inside of me when I reflected on the stations. I knew that the foundation of my faith was strong enough to hold all of my feelings and experiences because of

Christ's journey and his presence with me today. I have since walked the stations many times in many different locations, joining my journeys of suffering with Christ's, and each time I am so grateful for this deep companioning.

Listen. Find the stations of the cross at a monastery or church, in a book or online. As you "walk" or pray the stations, listen to the places in your life that have been touched by suffering.

Engage your body by walking as you gaze at the images. You might notice thoughts and feelings arising in you: those of betrayal, rejection, accusation, powerlessness, humiliation, falling, loneliness, loss, neediness or death. Pay attention to what is stirred inside of you. Notice what stations you are drawn to or to which ones you feel most resistant. Place your experiences into the experience of Jesus in the station that fits where you are spiritually and emotionally at that moment.

Connect with Jesus as you open to what comes by talking about, writing down or sketching your experience.

You may also journey for the suffering of another or simply enter into Jesus' historic journey and notice what comes. As Henri Nouwen reminds us, "There is no human pain or human joy that Jesus has not taken into himself."

Jesus too has fallen down.

- fourteen -

Grieve as We Can, Not as We Can't

To everything there is a season.

ECCLESIASTES 3:1 (KJV)

I LIVE IN SAN DIEGO; I have never understood seasons. Mine is a part of the country that likes to believe we can do anything we want any time we want and look good doing it. Productivity and appearance are highly valued, even in the church culture.

Something in me actually believes I am a better person when I get my lists accomplished, and if I can look good doing it, all the better! Sabbath, the concept of allowing my productivity to lie fallow in order to rest and remember that God is in charge, is both counterintuitive and countercultural. But when I'm not skipping through life, I need to remember that life is more than one shade of sunny. The blues and grays also belong.

Shortly after a friend of mine moved from California to Washington State, she found herself in a conversation with a Seattle woman about the weather. "Isn't Southern California like a woman who smiles *all the time*?" the woman asked. Her tone was tinged with disgust as she thought about my friend's former—and my current—excessively sunny environment. Honestly, I love the endless sun and surf.

Before we had our children, Joe and I spent a year living in Maine. That experience, so far from San Diego, taught me there actually is something annoyingly showy, pretentious really, about a seemingly "seasonless" climate endlessly prancing around in its fineries. It took time, but I came to love the seasons, gray ones and all.

The concept of seasons, I'm learning, can help us understand that at different times in life, different reactions and behaviors are appropriate, and not all of them will feel "like a woman who smiles *all the time*." In the spring, for example, flowers are blooming and trees are bearing fruit. Sometimes life looks beautiful and productive, and we find comfort in this. Other times life does not look so beautiful from the outside or feel so good on the inside.

Yet these times are natural and important parts of our lives as humans. As in winter, when many trees look dead and lifeless, things are often happening under the surface that we do not see or understand. There are times when dormancy allows roots to grow deeper into the soil. "Suffering produces endurance, and endurance produces character, and character produces hope," Romans 5:3-4 tells us. Can't you hear the roots deepening?

The author of Ecclesiastes understood this reality so long ago:

For everything there is a season, and a time for every matter under heaven:
  . . . a time to weep, and a time to laugh;
   a time to mourn, and a time to dance. (3:1, 4)

I am tempted to add:

  a time to smile and a time to frown.

The concept of church seasons, such as Advent, Lent and Ordinary Time, has also been helpful in giving me a foundation that holds all human experience as we place our journeys in Christ's journey. Lent has been particularly helpful in acknowledging and listening to loss.

This hasn't always been the case. In many Christian traditions, the word *hallelujah* is "hidden" or "buried" during Lent and not spoken again until Easter Sunday. I used to think the whole thing was odd, even a bit theologically questionable: Aren't we resurrection people? Shouldn't we be proclaiming hallelujah every day?

Now Lent is my favorite church season. In Lent, I am given permission to go against some of those smiley Southern California cultural expectations and allow myself to linger in a more reflective, thoughtful manner. This is not navel-gazing. Lent is a time of contrition and preparation. If I do not take the time to look inward and break the normal rhythms and ruts of spending money, consuming food and the ways I use and misuse my time, I will not know what it is that I should be contrite for. Fasting from things like the news, excessive food or drink, or social media exposes what has subtly gotten ahold of my heart and mind. Contrition for the hurts I've caused others and myself and for the life-draining patterns I have slipped into means that I must practice radical self-honesty and compassion in tending to what I discover.

Lent allows me to stop and listen to the griefs that have been neglected and gives me permission to tend to them. And the coming resurrection gives me the energy and hope to do this reflective work as I prepare for Easter Sunday and allow the pageantry of Holy Week to infuse this truth in my body.

Too Much to Grieve

Sometimes I think our worlds are too big and our exposure to tragedy goes beyond what our hearts are able to hold. Sometimes

I imagine living in a small town before the Internet, TV and cell phones. A child in town gets sick, a neighbor falls, someone loses his or her job. I imagine being able to do something tangible in an effort to tend to those difficult situations, whether it be cooking a pot of soup, being part of a prayer vigil, giving money, mowing a lawn or cleaning a home.

Now, in this big, complicated world, I often find myself pulling in the shutters. I have enough to deal with in my own home, and I have no idea what to do for the refugees of war, the hungry, the diseased, the orphans and widows. I don't hear about just one or two people in need; I hear about millions. We all do.

When I worked for Youth Specialties, a national youth ministry organization, I would receive emails regarding tragedies involving youth and youth leaders throughout the world. These tragedies weighed heavily on me in a way the tragedies revealed while listening to another in spiritual direction do not. I realized that spiritual direction allows me both to pray for the person in need and to do something to tend to that need, namely, listen to and companion the person in their suffering.

Receiving emails requesting prayer or other assistance from people outside of my close circle left me feeling overwhelmed and guilty for not doing more. Over the years, I began to tell my heart it's no good feeling that way, there is just too much need. In other words, I began a subtle disconnection between myself and the world. I didn't want to feel dread when I opened my email or glanced at the news; I wanted to feel *compassion*. I needed to find a way to listen to the hurts around me that I wasn't able to tend to directly and to release those situations into God's hands and care.

One way I've found is in Evening Prayer, a service outlined in the Episcopal Church's *Book of Common Prayer*.

Keep watch, dear Lord, with those who work, or watch, or
    weep this night,
and give your angels charge over those who sleep.
Tend the sick, Lord Christ:
give rest to the weary, bless the dying,
soothe the suffering, pity the afflicted,
shield the joyous; and all for your love's sake. Amen.

I discovered Evening Prayer when Joe and I moved to Maine to live near to Joe's former mentor, theater professor Jim Young. Known affectionately as "Jimma," he and his wife, June, were models to Joe and to me of faithfulness and love.

I watched Jimma react passionately to all the horrors on the nightly news. He carried the world deeply in his heart, and I was concerned about how this sensitive soul could engage so deeply in the world's woes and still wake up cheerful the next morning.

Then I figured out Jimma's secret: Evening Prayer. He poured out all his concerns to God in Evening Prayer, and when he was unable to do anything more, he left them there, trusting it was enough.

When a close friend of mine who lives far away was in crisis, Joe and I prayed this prayer with her for many weeks by phone. The situation was too much to bear. The nightly prayer brought us together, serving as a ritual of release and connection to the only One strong enough to hold the situation.

A TIME TO GRIEVE

Sometimes we fear falling apart. The reality is overwhelming, or too painful, and we want to run and hide. Sometimes our circumstances dictate a need to run and hide, stuffing our pain deep inside in order to feed our children, keep our jobs or not fall apart.

Laura's job the night Mark fell was not to grieve the diminishing vitality of her life partner; it was to keep her children feeling as safe and secure as possible while dealing with the unfolding reality.

"Tending our losses can be a luxury," my friend Martha, who did not have this "luxury" for a couple of difficult years, reminded me. She also reminded me that even when we are unable to tend our broken hearts, God tends them, perhaps through dreams, comforting lines of Scripture or poetry, the loving words and deeds of friends, wildflowers appearing in impossible places, and in ways we will never know.

We grieve what we need to grieve when we are ready, not what we think we are *supposed to* grieve or what others think we should grieve. The process cannot be forced. My favorite advice on prayer is attributed to Dom Chapman, a Benedictine spiritual director of the early 1900s: "Pray as you can, not as you can't."

This mirrors my best advice on grief: grieve as you can, not as you can't. The understanding of seasons, and with it, the realization that we don't need to appear happy and "fruitful" all the time—and, conversely, that we don't need to grieve everything all the time—has helped me grieve as I can, not as I can't.

PRAYER PRACTICE: *Evening Prayer with Jimma*

Jim Young and his grandson James created this version of Evening Prayer, taken primarily from *The Book of Common Prayer.*

Listen to Scripture, the prayers of the church, each other and your own heart.

Engage by gathering your family and friends to enter into a communal time of "letting go" together. Choose a leader and someone to read Scripture, then engage in all that you are carrying from the day by placing it within these prayers. This practice can also be done on your own.

Connect your hearts with God's heart as you pray this prayer together.

Evening Prayer

LEADER: The Lord Almighty grant us a peaceful night and a perfect end.

ALL: Amen.

LEADER: Our help is in the Lord.

ALL: Maker of heaven and earth.

LEADER: Let us confess our sins.

ALL: Almighty God, our heavenly Father:

We have sinned against you, through our own fault,

in thought, and word, and deed, and in what we have left undone.

For the sake of your Son, our Lord Jesus Christ,

forgive us all our offenses; and grant that we may serve you

in newness of life, to the glory of your Name. Amen.

LEADER: May the Almighty God grant us forgiveness of all our sins,

and grace and comfort of the Holy Spirit.

ALL: Amen.

READER: [*Scripture lesson selected*]

ALL: Keep watch, dear Lord, with those who work, or watch, or weep this night,

and give your angels charge over those who sleep.

Tend the sick, Lord Christ:

give rest to the weary, bless the dying,

soothe the suffering, pity the afflicted,

shield the joyous; and all for your love's sake. Amen.

ALL: [*Prayers of the People (A time to offer prayers about any-thing out loud)*]

LEADER: Let us pray the Lord's Prayer.

ALL: Our Father, who art in heaven, hallowed be thy name. Thy kingdom come, Thy will be done on earth, as it is in heaven. And forgive us our debts, as we forgive our debtors. Lead us not into temptation, but deliver us from evil. For Thine is the kingdom, the power, and the glory forever. Amen.

ALL: Awake may we watch with Christ, and asleep may we rest in peace.

Amen.

fifteen

Listening to the Shepherd

The Lord is my shepherd; I shall not want.

PSALM 23:1 (KJV)

WHY SHOULD I *not* want my shepherd?" I wanted to blurt out in the middle of Sunday school after the teacher finished reading Psalm 23—especially after she had spoken so highly of this shepherd. There he was on the flannelgraph with a sheep lovingly draped over his shoulder. What was even more confusing was that she read it straight out of the Bible, a book I had been taught to believe was trustworthy. It created in my young mind a crisis of faith. Do I listen to this authority figure *and* the Bible tell me that Jesus (who the flannelgraph shepherd looked an awful lot like) is someone I do *not* want, or do I decide quietly to keep believing what my heart was telling me—that I *do* want Jesus? I was confused but decided to trust my heart.

TRUST

Throughout our lives we learn who to listen to. We figure out who we can trust. I thought I had it down until the above incident with

Psalm 23 and Sunday school. And I continue to think I've got it straight—until I discover that I don't.

The practice of discernment, of listening deeply to God's presence and leading in and through our lives, is based in trust. If we do not trust in God's goodness and intimate involvement in our lives, we will not seek this guidance.

Trust is a casualty of loss. When I received the unwanted diagnosis of arthritis, trust in my body's strength and vitality was broken. When Joe and I thought our business venture was a dream come true and it turned into devastation, trust was shattered. When I believed I would receive a sense of God's presence in my darkest hours and I experienced silence, I lost some trust in my childhood Playmate.

When trust is broken, we often stop listening. I stopped listening to my body, both Joe and I stopped dreaming about our future, and I stopped believing God was beckoning me with delight around every bend.

Rest assured, I did eventually come to understand the Scripture as meaning the Lord is my Shepherd, I shall not *be in want* of anything else. That same Scripture, Psalm 23, goes on to paint a beautiful picture of how the Lord will lead us in places of peace and rest and to tables of provision even amidst our enemies. We can trust in this good Shepherd. I now love this Scripture (after I figured out that first part).

But when a sense of abandonment came in the midst of losing my brother, I lost trust that my Shepherd was all I needed. Was he really leading me beside still waters? And when we lost our business, I wondered, was he really providing for us, feeding us? Slowly I began to stop listening to the Shepherd who no longer seemed to be whispering to me.

I could not make trust happen. Trust happens when we are convinced of the trustworthiness of the other. All I knew to do was wait with broken trust, hoping that God would change something in my heart or understanding or circumstances that would allow me to open my ears and heart once again. I suppose I shouldn't be surprised that trust in God would be an issue from time to time, considering I've chosen to be in an intimate relationship with one I can't see and whose followers adhere to so many confusing and contradictory beliefs.

Thankfully, I had also read enough historic Christian literature to believe that God at times darkens our felt experience of God, classically known as the dark night of the senses and dark night of the soul. For reasons I will never fully understand that have to do with deepening our trust, purifying our hearts and stripping us of attachments, they are a necessary part of growth.

Grief Is Loud

In grief, when we are experiencing suffering, we often have internal and external voices coming at us from every direction, telling us what to do, telling us what we did wrong or telling us to "get over it." Grief is loud, and we don't have access to all our senses. That's why it is never a time to make important decisions when we are grieving.

This is where discernment comes in. As I was able to acknowledge the various losses, I slowly began to put my toe into the waters of trust. I realized that trust need not be blind. Blind trust is what I did when I was little and had no other choice. As an adult, I have the ability to think through things, to discern and to hold complexity. The Christian practice of discernment helps us recognize and distinguish God's promptings in us from the other kinds of promptings we tend to listen to, often unaware. It becomes crucial when I find myself in dark claustrophobic places. Fearful voices, cynical voices, judgmental voices, voices coming from my friends or friendly enemies, my culture, the wounded places within, come rising up, frantically vying for my attention.

I don't blindly trust anyone or anything, including my heart, mind, body, spouse or pastor. I am learning to listen deeply to hear the truth within these things, knowing that everything is tainted by imperfection in this "valley of the shadow of death" where we live out our lives. Everything also has the potential to be used and infused by the Spirit of God. God dwells in this valley. So, I ask, is there truth in this? And how is God present here?

Practicing discernment does not mean I will always get it right.

My mentor professor in spiritual direction, Dr. Elizabeth Patterson, railed against certainty when talking about the voice of God, admonishing us to proceed with humility. "It might be God," but, she'd say quoting Scrooge, "how do I know you're not 'just a bit of undigested beef'?"

Practicing discernment is also not the answer to never getting hurt again. It is a means of listening deeply to all of life in order to find and follow the divine whispers leading me home. So I might be, as Quaker author Thomas Kelly puts it, "stilled, tranquil, in child-like trust listening ever to Eternity's whisper, walking with a smile into the dark."

We are all God's ADHD children. We spend the majority of our time distracted from the things we most want to be paying attention to. When I taught school, one little girl in particular had trouble paying attention. I would walk up to her, put my hands gently on her face and direct her gaze to mine. Her face would light up in a smile and then she'd listen intently to the lesson. She wasn't trying to be bad; she just had a party going on in her head. Sometimes I can feel God hold my face, direct my gaze and say, "Here I am." This loving gaze is exactly where I want to be. Discernment to me is feeling God's hands on my face, directing me to God's gaze, so that I can receive and respond to love. "Oh, there you are!" I smile with relief.

PRAYER PRACTICE: *Discerning the Voices*

Discernment is discovering the ways the Shepherd speaks to us and has created each of us to recognize his voice (John 10). We all have negative "tapes" in our head and wounded places that speak into our situations. How do we sort out God's "still, small voice" from all the others?

Listen to the thoughts in your head, the things you tell yourself, the voices that dictate your behaviors. What are some of the things you hear yourself say that keep you from being honest about loss?

Engage. Notice your thought patterns around a loss you have experienced. (For me, it's things like, "Just get over it," "It's no big deal," "There's no point in bringing up old wounds.") Then ask yourself some questions:

1. Is this how God (Jesus, the Spirit) speaks to you?

2. Is the fruit of the Spirit present? If you are experiencing love, joy, peace, patience, kindness, goodness, faithfulness, gentleness or self-control, then the Spirit of God is probably at work (see Galatians 5:22).

3. How is your body feeling when you hear these voices (anxious, heavy, confused, irritated, defensive, shamed, open, connected, calm, relaxed, hopeful)?

4. Do you feel conviction or condemnation? (The Spirit convicts, other voices often condemn.) Conviction brings wholeness, often through repentance and realigning places where we have gotten off track. Condemnation is shaming. It shuts down our spirit and leads to hopelessness, not transformation.

5. As you begin to recognize the other voices that influence you, name them as you are able. (I have begun to recognize my inner drill sergeant, my inner critic and my inner victim.) Naming them can be a great way to take away their power.

Connect with God by recognizing the Shepherd's voice and allowing this voice to inform you more and more.

part three

INVITING HOPE

- sixteen -

Discoveries in the Dark

Darkness deserves gratitude.
It is the alleluia point at which we learn to understand
that all growth does not take place in the sunlight.

JOAN CHITTISTER

GREAT AUNT OLIVE WAS AN early explorer and promoter of the Carlsbad Caverns. One day, according to our family history, a group of government dignitaries arrived from Washington to determine if the caverns were worthy of National Monument status. They had no idea, however, that exploring them meant being lowered into the black void in an old guano mining bucket. As they stood hesitatingly peering over the edge into the dark abyss, Olive, who stood about four and a half feet tall with church shoes on, politely pushed her way through the crowd, hopped into the bucket and said, "Let's go, boys!" It worked of course. A tiny lady from New Mexico could not have more courage than big, important men from Washington, so down they all went, and the rest, as they say, is history. The park opened as a National Monument on October 25, 1923.

The caverns serve as a powerful symbol of some of the darkest places that lurk inside of me, places that come out in dreams or when my defenses are down. Places that feel too dark, too overwhelming, too bottomless.

It might just be the Holy Spirit, wearing a dress and a tight 1920s updo, who hops into my bucket and beckons me to accompany her into the darkness. I'm learning to trust that she will hold my hand and lead me exactly where I need to go, never leaving me and carrying all the light I need, "for darkness," the psalmist writes in 139:12, "is as light to you."

"God is not scared of our grief like we are," my wise therapist friend Tracy recently reminded me. "We are terrified of the intensity of our feelings while Jesus is saying, 'What else have you got? Bring it on, you are not too much for me.'"

Climbing into a bucket of bat guano and descending into the places that grief has opened in us is not a bad analogy. Our job, I believe, is to get into the bucket, to hold on and to notice what's being illuminated. It is the Spirit's job to guide the journey and do the illuminating. The Holy Spirit holds the flashlight.

DEEP IN THE DARKNESS

When I no longer felt like I was falling headlong into the abyss of depression, I started to look around. I began to discover what grief had illuminated on my cavern walls: fear, vulnerability and a terrifying sense of powerlessness lay underneath it all. I also began seeing glimpses of light along with other life forms in the darkness.

I discovered that fear had filled my calendar. Life felt out of control. Losing Mark and being unable to find stable places in my mind, and in my marriage, filled me with fear. My thinking was becoming rigid, self-protective and reactionary. This is a definition of fundamentalism. I began casting blame on others for the pain I was feeling: "If Joe would just do what he says he's going to do, I wouldn't feel so out of control." Compassion, which literally means to "suffer with," was not available to me in this dark state.

The experiences of loss and failure left me feeling vulnerable. I grew up on the classic fairy tales; men were strong, women and children were vulnerable, which meant weak and in need of rescue. I wanted to be Ponch from *CHiPs,* not Cinderella.

To be vulnerable is to be "susceptible to physical or emotional attack or harm," according to the web dictionary. Synonyms: "helpless, defenseless, powerless, impotent, weak," "open to being wounded." This is exactly what my fundamentalism was trying to protect me from. Vulnerability makes us feel out of control. And underneath fear and vulnerability, powerlessness reared its monstrous head. As I journeyed deeper into the dark cavern of grief, I discovered that powerlessness was the leviathan living in the abyss. Feelings of powerlessness are excruciating to me, like being forcefully held under water, unable to come up for air. It fills me with dread and triggers my escape mechanisms of blaming others and trying to regain control any way possible. I will fight or take flight in order to avoid these feelings.

ICONS OF HOPE

Two images pierced the darkness of this seemingly unending season of suffering. One had to do with breathing under water and the other with an awareness of darkness itself.

It dawned on me that I had not taken a deep breath for a year. My angry attempts to fight feelings of powerlessness were getting me nowhere. I couldn't hit the cancer that turned my brother into someone frightening to me before taking him away from us completely. I couldn't beat my fists at the recession that contributed to us losing our business. I couldn't strike a blow to my shattered marital expectations or my inability to handle what life was presenting to me. I was floundering, drowning, and I desperately needed to find a way to breathe under water. As soon as this cry formed in my spirit, something awoke in me: I am trained to breathe under water.

In high school I became a certified scuba diver. Breathing under water had opened up a whole world to me full of color and movement, mystery and wild creatures seen nowhere else. I knew then that I needed to stop waiting until circumstances changed and I surfaced. I needed to find my oxygen source there, under water. I began to consciously fill my lungs with the joys of my children, moments of beauty, my nightly bath and conversations with friends. I was still under water, to be sure, but I was beginning to breathe again.

I found myself drawn to whales. I began to spend a lot of time watching them in a nearby aquarium. Suffering feels like being swallowed up, trapped in a dark and claustrophobic place. I read about Jonah being swallowed by a "giant fish." I watched *Pinocchio* (both the Disney and VeggieTales versions) and repeatedly watched the part in *Finding Nemo* where Dory and Marlin get sucked into a whale. In each story, the whale represents a place of transformation. Jonah cried out to the Lord in surrender, Pinocchio became brave and honest, and Marlin learned to let go. They all thought they were going to die in that dark, underwater crucible, but instead they received exactly what they needed after spending time in that terrifying place.

The second icon of hope came from my own bookshelf as I pulled out a favorite copy of *The Cloud of Unknowing*, written by an unknown Christian mystic in the late Middle Ages. The book reminded me that God is intimately and mysteriously present in the dark. John of the Cross was there too, speaking to me from his poem "Dark Night of the Soul," a love song to the God who comes in the night. "Oh Night, that led me. . . . Oh Night far sweeter than the Dawn," it says. Many other saints and authors were there, right under my nose. These voices from the past were all telling me, "Do not fear the dark; look around."

I was learning to walk in the dark, as Barbara Brown Taylor phrases it. To me, this meant learning to engage in what my friend Angela calls the "unanswerable whys," the deep unknowns that lie at the heart of much suffering. Being present in the unanswerable whys meant holding the tension between how I believed things *ought to be* and how they *really were*. It meant feeling the fear and powerlessness that were lurking underneath my losses, letting the questions in, along with those unwelcome feelings, so that I could break the destructive cycle of my fear-based reactionary responses in order to accept what is.

In *When the Heart Waits: Spiritual Direction for Life's Sacred Questions,* Sue Monk Kidd quotes from her journal in the midst of a long, difficult season:

> Accept life—the places it bleeds and the places it smiles. That's your most holy and human task. Gather up the pain and the questions and hold them like a child upon your lap. Have faith in God, in the movement of your soul. Accept what is. Accept the dark.

I was beginning to see God in the dark and to remember that I love the dark. Darkness, after all, is a place of intimacy, as any lover or mystic knows.

GLIMPSES OF LIGHT

As my eyes adjusted to the dark, people began to appear in the corners of the cavern. Worlds opened up to which I had previously been blinded, or had dismissed or flippantly judged. And with this new seeing came compassion. Others were hurting too and needed help. And they too had things to teach me and gifts to give. My limited perspectives were being challenged. Stereotypes fell away—

I can no longer see a lawyer or person in the welfare line in the same dismissive way I did before being in crisis. I even see the jerk who cuts me off on the freeway or the scary-looking guy picking a fight outside the bar differently because I watched Mark's brain turn him momentarily into one of these people near the end of his life.

In the context of fear, to be vulnerable means to be susceptible to harm. In the context of compassion, to be vulnerable means to be susceptible to beauty and goodness, to God and all the manifestations of love. It means we are susceptible to a sunset overwhelming our senses, to that perfect piece of music transporting us to the heavenly realms, to a kiss awakening us so that the mere memory of it makes us smile.

I used to think vulnerability was a design flaw that allowed for hurt to penetrate the open places that were made to let love and joy in, but now I'm not so sure it's a flaw. Tracy, my therapist friend, puts it this way:

> We seem to be created to get our hearts broken. That is the consequence of love. Our broken hearts remind us of our need: our need for God mainly and our need for each other. Our broken-heartedness is the pathway to compassion. It allows us to remember our basic humility and humanity. It is not the exception but the rule. Our culture is so very backward about this honest truth.

Darkness is defining. Inviting hope means finding the courage to explore the darkness. When I don't have any, I'm learning to cling to someone who does. I cling to the story of my Great Aunt Olive like a neoprene wetsuit. She helps me journey forward, even when forward looks a lot like going down. Inviting hope means getting into the bucket.

How was I going to come out of this crucible? Not more defensive and rigid, I hoped, not more of a fundamentalist, but more of a mystic, caught up in the mysteries of God that lie beyond my senses, and more of a lover, moved by God and others through my senses, both roles connecting me to life on an intimate level.

PRAYER PRACTICE: *Centering Prayer*

Find a way to breathe under water. Discover what allows you to sink into the deeper reality of God so that your chest starts to expand again. It might be sitting in a coffee house with a good book, staring at a favorite painting at an art museum, going for a long walk or having a nightly phone conversation with a good friend.

Centering prayer became a vital means of breathing under water during the last year of Mark's life and has continued to be a meaningful prayer practice for me. In centering prayer I am simply breathing and allowing myself to be "calmed and quieted . . . like a weaned child with its mother." This image from Psalm 131 is the crux of my prayer as I desire to rest in God's presence underneath all of my thoughts, images, feelings and agendas. My intention is to surrender to God.

It's interesting that my other favorite image for centering prayer is to be under water but this time held comfortably in the silence and mystery of God, able to receive God's very breath in me. From that standpoint, I watch the waves of thoughts, feelings and activities churn up the surface of the sea, and I choose to let them go for the time being and return to this deep, abiding Presence. I am constantly moving between distraction and abiding, and this is just fine. My breath and intention brings me back.

Listen, and ask God to give you a word or image that will help you focus your attention and intention on God. Choose something simple and short, like Jesus, Abba, Come Lord, yes, or an image like a child held on his or her mother's lap.

Engage and connect in this practice of silent prayer, resting and abiding. When distractions come, silently say your sacred word, renewing your desire to be with God. Use your word as often as needed. (Instead of a sacred word, when a distraction comes, I envision God filling my lungs with breath.)

This prayer practice is often done daily for twenty or thirty minutes, but even five minutes a day can be a gift.

- seventeen -

Letting the Light In
Through Nature and Beauty

*If eyes were made for seeing, then beauty
is its own excuse for being.*

RALPH WALDO EMERSON

*The cure for anything is saltwater-
sweat, tears or the sea.*

ISAK DINESEN

A BRILLIANT STREAK OF YELLOW shocked me out of my daze on the day I drove to the hospital where my brother lay in a medically induced coma. The freeway onramp was overwhelmed by wildflowers I had not noticed before. Time was suspended as I rounded the corner surrounded by gray, dirty concrete and a blur of cars speeding by. All I could see was yellow. Such an inappropriately joyful color. Each time I drove by them after that, often heading to the sterile room full of sights and emotions I did not want to see, they cheered and danced and sang as I passed.

How odd, I thought, that beauty still exists.

We celebrated the first Christmas after Mark's brain herniated in the rehab hospital. We had hoped and prayed that Mark could come home for Christmas, but we'd had no idea how extensive the damage was to his brain. That Christmas night, as I entered the freeway to drive the short distance home, I was surprised by joy. I looked through my windshield to see what appeared to be the letters J-O-Y, coming out of the lighted windows on the side of a hotel. I laughed, believing my eyes were playing tricks on me. It was the last thing I could feel at that moment, Christmas or no Christmas. But as I got closer, the word became clearer. The entire side of a twelve-story hotel read "JOY." It turns out the owners don't book out the eighty-five rooms that face busy Mission Valley during the Christmas season so they can manipulate the room lights and send that message.

Every night as I tried to catch my breath after leaving Mark in the rehab hospital, there it was. This hotel held the joy for me that I was unable to hold for myself. It reminded me that joy, like beauty, still exists in the darkness.

"The eyes are the windows to the soul," the English proverb states, and I believe it. Sometimes it is the beauty of an art museum that helps let the light in. I am fortunate to live blocks from Balboa Park, a beautiful piece of Eden, holding San Diego's finest museums. I have my favorite paintings—including the *Young Shepherdess* by William-Adolphe Bouguereau—that beckon me or the small works of Christ's life by Georges Rouault, but mostly when I'm feeling beauty-deprived and world-weary, I like to wander in a noncommittal fashion, open to whatever painting wants to flirt with me, feed me with its beauty or touch something in me that needs touching through its colors or content. I breathe more deeply, no longer taking in those tiny, shallow gasps of air that I hadn't noticed I had been taking for I don't know how long. I go home having my claustrophobic, pain-induced perspectives enlarged.

Letting beauty in through our eyes does to the mind what letting fresh air in does to the body: it creates the space needed to heal. "There is a crack in everything God has made," Emerson writes, and Leonard Cohen adds, "That's how the light gets in."

NATURE

A few years after Joe and I were married, a person who was important to me was killed in a car accident. Two weeks later, I found myself at a five-day silent retreat in the Maryland woods. Ironically, the person killed, my boss Mike Yaconelli, was the very person who had approved and paid for me to go on this retreat. Somehow in the crazy divine workings, Mike had sent me on the week of intense grieving I needed in order to come back and serve his beloved company, Youth Specialties, as a spiritual director in their time of deep grief.

By sitting in silent prayer with others and taking long walks in the snowy woods, I began to let some of the internal chatter begging for attention come to the surface. For hours, I held late night conversations with God and Mike, the moon and the snow-covered bridge over the frozen pond outside my window. I yelled, wept, questioned and complained. I grieved myself empty.

After I woke from my exhausting and cathartic first night, I pulled on my jacket and boots and set out for the woods. I walked and walked, without destination, allowing my body to work out the trauma trapped inside. In a clearing, I found myself standing in front of a dead deer, its body decomposing. At first I was disturbed by this grotesque image, but instead of wanting to leave, I felt drawn to stay. I sat next to that deer for hours, returning each day. I didn't understand why but knew that next to this decaying deer is where I needed to be.

In his profound and personal book *The Solace of Fierce Landscapes*, Belden Lane writes of finding grace in the grotesque. To discover God's presence in brokenness, weakness and despair we need to admit that "grace rarely comes as a gentle invitation to change. More often than not it appears in the form of an assault, something we first are tempted to flee."

Do not pass by on the other side of the street. It is in a disfigured person, a tortured and torturing soul that you might recognize something of yourself and even see glimpses of the divine.

Nature, even in its harshest most unforgiving forms like the deer I sat with, holds life. I felt myself slowly being enfolded in a greater reality of the life-death-life cycle. As I sat with the devastated remains of the deer, I was able to acknowledge the reality that this is what we are left with in the present, the hard and horrible, ugly and unwanted journey of losing someone we love. And I felt in my late-night conversations with God and Mike that Mike was fine, more alive than he had ever been before. Both realities were somehow true.

Saltwater

For me, the most powerful form of healing through nature has come in the form of saltwater. Twice a week the ocean holds me and lets me dance and play in its energy, energy that started thousands of miles away and ends in the wave I ride. The ocean doesn't care if I am happy or sad. It teaches me through its consistency—endless waves lapping one after another on the shore and tides ebbing and flowing twice a day.

It also teaches me through its inconsistent, unpredictable nature. I have surfed twice a week at the same spot for the past twenty years, and each time the scene is different, both the landscape, as the wave size and direction along with tides produce an ever-changing geography, and the flora and fauna.

Sometimes I surf with dolphins, seals, leopard sharks, stingrays and schools of fish. Sometimes seaweed entangles me, hooking my board's fin, and I go flying off the wave. The ocean reminds me that I can work with, live in and even play in both the consistency and inconsistency of nature. Surfing gives me hope that I can learn to ride the waves of life with increasing grace and skill, surrender and joy.

I can also visit beluga whales at the aquarium when I want to be close to saltwater. When I first discovered the belugas, I fell in love. I sat mesmerized, watching their sleek white bodies move gracefully through the water. I was particularly drawn to the contrasts of light and dark that played out on their massive bodies as rays of light filtered down from above. This touched the part of me that was trying to hold both the hopes and disappointments around our challenging fertility journey. Watching them became my most helpful prayer practice. Their beauty would penetrate my heart, calm my mind and somehow cause me to know, deeply know, that all would be well, regardless of how our fertility story unfolded.

When I'm not able to be in the ocean and I need to feel grounded and held by something larger than myself, I can open my front door and step outside. I live in the basement of a large Craftsman-style home in Bankers Hill, a historic neighborhood just above downtown San Diego. It's small and not very practical, but every window and door of our home opens onto a magical canyon. I say magical because I am pretty sure fairies live there, though I haven't actually seen one yet.

My family and I eat our meals on the deck surrounded by huge eucalyptus trees and various canyon critters. Raccoons, skunks, squirrels, foxes and possums have all come to visit. I shoo the kids into the canyon with snacks and a safety whistle. "Whistle if you are in danger," I tell them. And I watch them from above, tiny little specks of color bravely exploring their world. My heart is overwhelmed with love.

Are you watching me like this, God?

PRAYER PRACTICE: *Nature Walk*

One very practical lesson I've learned in dealing with loss is to pay attention to what I see and how I see. I do not need to be a passive recipient of the thousands of images the advertising agencies flash in front of my eyes or the images my internal thoughts flash in my mind. I am learning to bring intentionality to my visually saturated world, to contemplate what I see.

Contemplation means to look at something thoughtfully, slowly and with love. Learning to see with love and be touched by what I see has become an important practice. Nature provides the perfect tableau.

Find a special place in nature. This can be a small city park, a vast desert wilderness or any place in between.

Listen to your heart, thoughts and body as you journey to your nature spot.

Engage and connect. Take a long, slow walk, pouring out your thoughts and feelings as you walk in one direction. When you feel you have poured yourself empty, acknowledging and sharing all that is within you to share, turn around. As you walk back, simply open your eyes and heart to the surrounding beauty. Allow God to touch you through the things being presented to your senses. Breathe. Look, listen, smell, feel the world around you. Stop when something catches your eye, explore, meander, be curious. If you need help, watch a child explore nature and do what they do. Get your feet wet, walk barefoot, stomp in a puddle, feel the breeze, lie in the tall grass, whatever the invitation might be. Enjoy!

- eighteen -

Cathartic Creativity

Jack-asses
Surrounded by jack-asses Who continually bray
"He is in heaven"
"It is time to move on"
"Where is your faith"
"This is God's plan"
"Get over it"
"Don't you trust God"

God deliver me from these beasts of burdens
Their words crush me their words arise from an ignorance of You
An ignorance of me

O God, In your grace and mercy
Smack them over the head with a 2 by 4

LARRY WARNER

THERE ARE ENDLESS creative ways to grieve. My friend Larry began writing poetry after his son was killed. Shortly after Mark became ill, Laura began to paint. For some, it's restoring an old car, playing an instrument, refinishing furniture, starting a new hobby or developing a new skill.

During my freshman year of college when my father resigned from pastoring our church and he and Mom prepared to move two hundred miles away, I would sneak back into the hallowed sanctuary of the church that had embraced me since I was eighteen months old. I would turn on the spotlights that illuminated the altar and grand piano, and I'd sit and play that majestic instrument alone, eyes closed, allowing all that was in my heart to channel through my fingers onto the keys and out into the universe. My cries, the ones I was only able to utter through the piano keys, echoed through that sacred place, and I was heard and held in a divine embrace.

Creativity, in whatever form we choose, brings energy to our bodies and opens up new places within us. We might discover longings and giftedness that we had never given ourselves permission to explore before. Pain is often the great motivator behind big and small works of art, whether Van Gogh's masterpieces or the planting of a garden.

MAKING AND BREAKING THINGS

Breaking things—really smashing them—can also be a cathartic way to grieve and has helped me let out pent-up negative energy. Breaking things feels really good after loss has broken our hearts or dreams or expectations. It's not the best idea, however, to break things we will regret, such as our bodies, smartphones or someone else's heart.

When I worked in a residential treatment facility with emotionally disturbed teenagers, we kept a stack of phone books on hand for kids to rip to shreds when they were overcome by anger. This is a great way for *any of us* to channel emotional pain. The kids would exhaust themselves instead of hurting themselves or others. The torn-up paper symbolized the shredded mess of what they felt inside.

Once, during a spiritual direction session, as the person I was meeting with was sharing areas of deep grief, I became aware of our surroundings. We were meeting on the deck of a cheerful seaside restaurant, sun shining down and a pretty flower in the vase between us. I felt the dissonance of her internal landscape and the external environment, like we were being hovered over by a woman who smiles *all the time*. So I took the flower out of the vase, bent down and, as subtlety as possible, smashed the vase against the table leg, then placed the shattered glass pieces between us. I have no idea if my act of breaking the vase and the symbolism of the shattered pieces helped my directee, but it helped me. (On the way out I asked if I could pay for the glass vase I had broken. When the staff refused, I dropped a five in the tip jar.)

Inanimate material objects, I recognize, do matter. A car, computer, favorite book or dish often hold meaning and represent things far beyond the worth or purpose of the objects themselves. When these things crash or break or disappear, we experience loss.

One day while at my folks' house, my mom pulled me aside with tears in her eyes. She had broken one of her china dishes, the "fancies" with the delicate lilac pattern passed down from her mother. Mom was having trouble coming to terms with her "clumsiness." Before I left that night, I secretly pulled the dish out of the trashcan. The next morning, I cracked the dish into small pieces, bought a wooden "lazy Susan" and proceeded to turn my mom's sad mistake into a revolving tray with her beautiful china piece creating a mosaic on top. Mom loved it, very sincerely, I believe, not just in the way moms love four-year-old crayon drawings that hang on the refrigerator for far too long.

Writing a Parable

One of the most surprisingly healing acts of creativity came while attending a retreat called "Writing the Parables of Our Lives" at Saint Andrew's Abbey. My fellow participants and I were handed one of Christ's parables and instructed to write whatever came to mind. "Parables do not tell us how to think or what to believe," the leaders reminded us. "They are meant to confound our black-and-white thinking and draw us into a deeper truth."

Suffering is like a parable. It confounds our brains and cannot be worked out cleanly. We are left to ask, "Is there a deeper meaning? A way through? A loving Presence in the midst?" This writing assignment helped me notice the sacred parable being revealed through the story of my life during a time when I was unable to see much of anything.

I was given the parable from Matthew 20:1-16 about the land-owner who hired laborers early in the morning to work his vineyard and agreed to pay them a denarius a day. At the third and sixth hour, he saw people "standing idle in the marketplace" and hired them. At the eleventh hour he found others and said, "Why have you been standing here idle all day?" They told him they hadn't been hired, so he hired them. At the end of the day he gathered the workers and paid them all the same amount: one denarius.

The ones who worked all day complained, but the landowner answered, "Did you not agree with me for a denarius? . . . I wish to give to this last man the same as to you. Is it not lawful for me to do what I wish with my own things?" The parable ends by saying, "So the last will be first, and the first last. For many are called, but few chosen" (NKJV).

This parable did not seem to apply to my life, so I set it aside. In the middle of the night, this parable came to me:

For the kingdom of heaven is like this—a woman did not know how to pay her bills. She and her husband had both lost their stable sources of employment. With two young children to tend to, it was agreed that the children would be her labor and her husband would look for employment outside the home, both believing they were capable and God would provide.

The husband, however, was not as proactive in his pursuit as the woman had hoped. As days turned to weeks, and weeks turned to months of watching him *stand idle in the marketplace*, her anxieties and confusion mounted. "Where are you, God?" she would cry.

The woman had a brother, her only sibling, who had become seriously ill. Days turned to weeks, weeks to months, months to years. As prayers for healing went unanswered, her anxieties and confusion mounted, and an overwhelming sense of scarcity, an unknown experience up until this season, settled deep within her spirit. "Where are you, God?" she would cry.

When the brother's wife had to return to work and was no longer able to care for her ailing husband, the parents took him into their home.

In what now felt to the woman certainly to be the eleventh hour, she said to her husband, "Why have you been standing here idle all day, week, month, year?"

"Because no one has hired me," he responded.

The aging parents hired the woman's husband to care for their son. The husband cared for his brother-in-law with tenderness and compassion, living in his in-laws' home three days a week for a year. He slept alongside his brother-in-law, walked with him, read to him, bathed him, all the while masterfully navigating the woman's family dynamics, bringing care to her brother and comfort to her parents.

Yet still there was concern over finding stable employment, still deep worries for the woman. Still confusion over God's presence in all of this. She was no longer able to utter her prayer of "Where are you, God?" A sense of abandonment had unpacked its bags in her soul.

Then, *way* beyond the *eleventh hour*, from what felt like out of the blue, her husband was offered a meager quarter-time job in his field. At the end of the day, this insufficient offering turned into a full-time job with benefits.

One month later, the woman's husband spent the day tenderly caring for her brother who was now confined to his bed. The next day, her husband began his new job. And the following morning, her brother took his last breath.

Consider this.

PRAYER PRACTICE: *Make or Break Something*

Two suggestions:

1. Make a collage. This practice was not at all interesting to me until I did it. I have created a handful of collages over the years, and each time the experience has been powerful.

Listen to what is inside of you asking for attention.

Engage what you find by making a collage. Get a stack of magazines and a half sheet of paper (thicker paper is good, and I've found the containment of a half sheet is helpful). Prayerfully look through and cut out any images and words you are drawn to and glue them onto the paper.

Connect. Use what you have created as a future prayer tool, or simply allow the practice of creating and noticing to be your prayer.

You might want to ask yourself, *Where am I experiencing loss or disconnection right now?* Create a collage around this on one side of the paper, and then on the other side create a collage by asking, *Where am I experiencing peace and connection right now?*

2. Make a mosaic or just break some dishes.

Mosaic making is one of my favorite creative ways to grieve. When I break something I love, I can turn it into something else I love. Or I can go to Goodwill, buy twenty dollars' worth of ceramic dishes, wildly smash them onto the ground, and allow my mind and muscles to work out pent-up anger from some hurt I've received. (I make sure the kids aren't around when I do this.) Then I sweep up the pieces and either throw them all away or create something beautiful.

So listen, engage and connect as you make something, break something, or both.

nineteen

Feeding Jesus Doughnuts

When life confronts us with our limits,
those who have lived with limits all their
lives instruct us most profoundly.

BELDEN LANE

F OR TWO YEARS I FED Jesus doughnuts every Friday morning and Monday afternoon. Sometimes Jesus didn't like the doughnut I had chosen for him and asked me to go back into the hefty bag to locate one with sprinkles or more glaze. I'd usually comply. At times Jesus said, "Thank you," other times he was silent or offered me his gap-toothed grin. Sometimes Jesus was downright rude, but that was okay. It's hard to keep your sense of humor when you've had to sleep, night after night, on cold concrete with only a thin piece of cardboard as your bed.

Ever since I was a child, I've heard the words of Jesus from Matthew 25, "For I was hungry and you gave me food, I was thirsty and you gave me something to drink" (v. 35), but it wasn't until the two years I spent helping fill Jesus' growling stomach and supporting his sugar addiction that I really understood. Those two years coincided with the most arduous part of our fertility journey. Those years found me sticking needles into my own stomach and developing a deeper respect for what had become second nature to my diabetic husband. That was a time where everything felt on hold, our future unknown, and life itself fragile and complicated. My work in the soup kitchen in downtown San Diego was one of the most helpful ways of making it through this difficult period. Being with people who knew pain and suffering gave me courage to look at my own.

When Mark was first diagnosed with brain cancer, I was a new mother. The amount of service involved in motherhood was overwhelming, yet it was through feeding my daughter, changing a diaper, washing bottles and the myriad of other new tasks presenting themselves to me that I began to work out the thoughts and emotions that overwhelmed my mind and heart. My own debilitating isolation and despair were held at bay through these acts of service to my daughter.

Of course, for some people, helping others becomes an excuse to *not* deal with their own pain. We can use the great needs we find around us to distract us from grief and activate our tendency to minimize our own sufferings ("They don't even have a home, why on earth should I take time to focus on my own little difficulty?"), or we can use the compassion we feel for others to help us find compassion for ourselves. We can use our sufferings to feel solidarity with all who suffer. Through feeding hungry people, I was learning how to give and receive.

SEEING AND SERVING

When Mark and I were growing up, our church would visit the local convalescent hospital. We would serve the elderly in our community by singing, visiting and lighting up their day in whatever ways we could think of. Most of the other children shied away from these folks, confined to their beds or wheelchairs, who couldn't play catch or cards anymore or do anything meaningful with a child. I was a bit frightened of them, too, and the place smelled bad.

Mark, a born historian, loved old things—including old people. He would march up to someone that no one else dared to even glance at, take his or her hand and begin asking questions. He knew that underneath the sometimes frightening façade was a person who held a lifetime of experiences that no one else held, and he wanted to hear these stories. Mark took a deep interest in the person in front of him. He valued them, which of course was the best kind of service possible. I went home feeling good about myself, checking off my "I did a good thing today" box and happy to not return for a few weeks. Mark went home filled and satisfied, wanting to return the next day, caring nothing about the jewels in his crown.

He taught me what it really means to serve. To give and to receive from another. To see value in the other and to find the doorway into meaningful connection. When I really understand that Jesus is in the "least" of these, serving becomes an act of worship and connection with God, something that is designed to fill and not deplete.

By serving my infant daughter and my homeless neighbors, I was given a constant reminder of a bigger world that needed my attention and care. As I began to see with compassion the value of the other in front of me, something opened in me, and I started to receive warmth, smiles and stories that filled me and touched my depleted soul. Serving others in this way became a means of engaging in my own story of grief and a surprising channel of healing and restoration.

PRAYER PRACTICE: *Praying with the Least of These*

Listen to the places of poverty and neglect in your own heart, mind and body. What are the displaced, devalued places inside of you that seek compassionate attention? Loss often brings these places to the surface. If this terminology is not helpful, simply recognize that there are places of need and hurt inside of you.

Engage. Find a person or group whom the world might consider the "least of these" and engage with them in meaningful ways. This could include feeding the hungry, visiting the sick or lonely, helping the elderly or disabled, or caring for a child. Whatever you do, seek to give value to the other. The best way to do this is to offer them your full listening attention and compassionate presence. Everyone has this to give.

Connect with the other through your meaningful engagement, and as you do, see the eyes of Jesus shining through the other's eyes. Allow yourself to give and to receive.

- twenty -

Sacred Symbols

*We too must carry our cross in
order to share in the fruits of the redemption;
consequently we need a very vivid image
before our minds at all times.*

FROM SELF-TOUR COMMENTARY FOR GUIDO RENI'S
Christ with the Crown of Thorns at the Getty Museum

SYMBOLS CAN BE MEANS of grace in times of grief. One day in the midst of double unemployment, mounting debts and an unknown financial future, a friend, Lilly, stayed at our house. When she left she handed me a bar of handmade soap as a thank-you gift. I placed the soap in my soap dish and thought nothing more about it—until about two months later.

The soap, which the four of us used multiple times a day in our only bathroom, looked the same as it had when I'd peeled off the brown paper wrapping. How strange, I thought. We usually go through soap quickly. Every day after that, I watched the soap seemingly replenish itself. We scrubbed and it lasted.

"Abundance," the soap persistently whispered, in a year filled with scarcity. It reminded me of the little jar of oil in 2 Kings 4 that continued to pour out, giving the widow and her children what they needed to survive. That little bar of soap became the symbol for me that God's abundance was still present. It lasted the entire year.

Symbols have been significant means of helping me engage my grief. Some come to me as gifts, others I discover or create. Symbols are very personal things. I know a symbol is meaningful when my heart is drawn to it and it brings a sense of hope or help.

I light a white votive candle, my "Christ candle," as a wordless prayer when the darkness is too dark and I have no idea how to pray. The light becomes a symbolic reminder of God's presence in the midst of tragedy. I light it to keep vigil with the person who is suffering. I light it when a loved one dies, symbolically illuminating his or her final journey. I lit my candle recently for Chiyoko, for Veronica, for Grandma Doris and for Anne. I light it when I feel helpless in the face of tragedy, as I did when a sick man entered Sandy Hook Elementary School and killed twenty-six people, twenty of them children the same age as mine. I lit it as a reminder that they were not alone, that Jesus was present amidst the darkest darkness. The prayer continues rising up through the night while I sleep. This helps.

I clung to symbols with all my might in the season of Mark's illness.

Tasting the Vinegar

While on retreat and praying the Stations of the Cross, I found myself at the tenth station, where Jesus is stripped of his garments. My friend Lilly had designed the stations for use in prayer and had placed a earthenware cup of vinegar at station ten with the written suggestion that we take a sip, reminding us of the bitter pain Jesus experienced on his way to the cross. I was drawn to that station alone.

As I held the cup, I could see Mark, stripped, lying on a gurney in his hospital gown. I began to name all that was being stripped from him. Then I began to focus on my own stripping: stripped of my brother, my job, financial security, illusions of control, beliefs about God. As I stared at the image of Christ, I was being invited to feel the relentless stripping of his, Mark's and my own journeys.

When I came home from the retreat, I poured some vinegar into the Van Gogh–blue chalice I'd bought at a market deep in Mexico and placed it above the kitchen sink. Next to the cup I leaned a small metal relief of Jesus on the cross that Mark had found in an antique store and given to me. Every day for several months, I took a sip of the bitingly bitter stuff as a prayer, reminding me that pain and loss are part of my journey today, and as an encouragement to accept the journey with God's help rather than pretend it's not as bitter as it actually is.

At some point during those few years when Mark was still with us, yet not entirely, another friend, Libbie, gifted me with a crucifix she had bought in the monastery we both love. She placed the small wooden cross with a silver Christ figure in my hand and instructed me to hold on to Jesus. "He is close to us in the dark," she said. Growing up, I was taught to focus on the fact that Jesus is no longer on the cross. "He is risen. He is risen indeed!" What I needed, though, as Libbie knew, was to draw near to the Jesus who suffered and who draws near to us in our suffering.

Yes, I need an image of the suffering Christ before me as well as the risen Christ because both represent my journey and the realities of faith and life. When I had to "carry my cross" and be led in places I did not want to go, like the bankruptcy court or the hospice hospital, I would put the crucifix in my pocket and feel the Christ figure against my palm. And many nights when overcome by anxiety, I would hold the crucifix in my hand. Without words, I was asking Jesus to take onto the cross the darkness I was experiencing.

This helped.

HONORING LOSS

I have heard it said that Franklin Delano Roosevelt was among the last Americans who wore the black armband publicly after his mother died. In many cultures, people who grieve wear black for a period of time, often a year. In America, this was tapered down to a simple black armband worn on the upper arm.

After Mark died, I found myself wishing we still had a similarly public symbol. So many of us at any given time are limping around, silently grieving a devastating loss and all the while trying to keep up appearances of normalcy. But what if there were this subtle symbol, cluing us in to the painful reality of a fellow human being. We might be a little more patient at the grocery store when this person is fumbling distractedly in her purse while the checkout line builds behind her. It would force us to stop pretending that everything is okay and evoke the compassion that naturally comes when we realize that many of us are dealing with much more than meets the eye.

I went online and found a company that still sells the black bands and ordered a few. When I feel the weight of grief, I wear the band under my clothes. I've found that this physical reminder allows me to honor the emotional realities in a way that helps carry and relieve some of the weight. In a similar way, when I am acutely feeling Mark's absence or desire to feel his presence, I wear his sweater or one of the many other pieces of clothing he'd passed to me through the years.

The Bible offers us plenty of ways to creatively engage with loss through symbolism, ritual and raw emotion. In Esther, we see sackcloth and ashes. In 1 Kings, we see tearing of clothes. Job sits with friends in the custom of sitting Shiva, as Jews still do today after a death. Esau, Jacob, Joseph, David, Jesus and many more choose to weep and wail. Symbols and rituals become our buckets or containers that allow the deep places within to come into the light and be transformed.

PRAYER PRACTICE: *Create a Space of Remembrance*

Mark and I loved to venture to Mexican cemeteries during Dia de los Muertos, or Day of the Dead. We'd watch families make altars and decorate graves with photos, marigolds and sugar skulls, then share stories about their loved one in laughter and tears. We liked the way the dead were remembered and celebrated instead of never spoken about or spoken of only in hushed tones. In college, when our dog Tippy died, Mark found a picture of Tippy and made it into a creative art piece. Now we add Mark's picture to the Dia de los Muertos altar at my kids' Spanish-immersion school and to the space of remembrance at our church during All Souls' Day.

Listen to what kind of space you desire to create in or around your home. This could be a prayer closet, a sacred space of rest and connection with God. It could be a place of remembrance honoring a lost loved one. It could be a "wailing wall" that physically holds multiple prayers and griefs. One of my favorite books, *The Secret Life of Bees* by Sue Monk Kidd, has a character that feels the world deeply. She has a wailing wall out back where she tucks little pieces of paper. Each piece holds a prayer that she can no longer carry.

Engage. Create your sacred space, dedicating a corner, closet, table or section of a wall to God. Do you need pillows, a special blanket, a rocking chair, some kind of cloth drapery, candles, photos or items of loved ones who have passed away, or other things that symbolize losses, bricks or rocks, pieces of paper to write down prayers? Look up images of sacred spaces and get creative.

Connect as you pray, listen, rest or wrestle with God in your sacred space.

twenty-one

Ritual and Healing

*"I don't feel very much like Pooh today," said Pooh.
"There, there," said Piglet. "I'll bring you
tea and honey until you do."*

A. A. MILNE,
Winnie-the-Pooh

EVERY SUNDAY MORNING my husband and I wake up and invite our two little ones into bed for a family snuggle. Then we start to get ready for church, which abruptly dissolves any good feelings we've gained from snuggle time. There are at least two breakdowns, one almost always being mine. Joe prays during our five-minute drive to church, with the rest of us occasionally adding an offering or two. I mostly look out the window and anxiously wonder whether Joe notices the car in the lane we're merging into.

Once at church, I stand and confess in the presence of my brothers and sisters; I listen to the Scriptures and the words of the pastor. In the liturgical prayers, I pray for things I would not normally pray for, like our political leaders, and ask the Lord for things I usually forget to ask for, such as to care for the poor. I speak out loud the names of people on my heart—aging parents, hurting friends, sometimes I whisper my own name—feeling the whole congregation holding them, holding me, up to God.

I stand with others in whatever state of faith or doubt I happen to be in. And as we say together the statements about God we hold true, I am held in the faith of the congregation regardless of my current thoughts and feelings. Then we "pass the peace," many of us, including the pastor and our little ones—who have now joined us in "Big Church"—making the entire rounds before settling in for a very disruptive second half of the service. The kids wiggle and squirm and say inappropriate things like "I just pooted!" just as the entire congregation drops into silent prayer.

Then we partake in Communion, which somehow even the youngest of us, or perhaps especially the youngest of us, knows is sacred. When our son, Akian, was two, he would hit the floor running. Hands cupped to receive the special bread of Jesus, he'd attempt to dodge around the more staid Lutherans who were patiently waiting their turn. I had to pull him back two or three times. Allena, at three, would walk just in front of us, slowly, thoughtfully, hands cupped, ready to receive the precious bread of Jesus' body with a pious expression she must have seen on one of those Christmas cards of Mary and Jesus that come free in the mail.

I watch our pastor bend low to feed my children the bread of life. Then he hands me a chunk of bread, looks me in the eye and says, "This is Christ's body. May he heal you and bring you everlasting life." I drink from the cup of wine and hear the words spoken over me, "This is Christ's blood," and I respond, "Amen," and even in the darkest hour, I know that it is and that somehow it is enough.

Then it all goes downhill from there. The kids start begging for the goodies in the foyer. They run loudly back and forth to the kids' basket, grabbing books they refuse to sit still long enough to read. Or if they do read, their voices are louder than the pastor's closing prayers. Finally I grab a child and head for the door or give Joe the look that says, "It's your turn." Then, just as I'm feeling the need to go around apologizing to everyone for my disruptive offspring, Irmgard directs her walker in my direction. When she reaches me she grabs my hand and says, "Oh, how I love the children. They are *our* children, you know." And I can see in her eyes that she means it.

All of this makes up one of the most important rituals in my life. At times, church is the last place I want to be, particularly when I'm feeling depressed. But I have learned to come anyway, and I leave knowing I am part of something greater than myself. My community holds the faith with me and sometimes *for* me when I am unable to hold it myself. This cynical, church-weary soul has heard the whispers of Eden through the communal ritual of worship in this beautiful, quirky, imperfect place, and I am so grateful.

We love the rich pageantry our church embraces during Holy Week. We wave palm branches, wash each other's feet, pray the Stations of the Cross and sit in the darkness, all culminating in a long Easter vigil, where we hear the Scripture's stories of our faith around a makeshift campfire, process around the block by candlelight and return to our now fully illuminated church. Out come our hallelujahs (a word we had "hidden" during all of Lent), along with the various musical instruments we'd brought from home, and the Easter celebration begins.

The Easter after Mark died, I remember feeling a deep dissonance with the rituals. Engaging in this journey with my faith community leads me to *feel* the resurrection in my bones. But not that year. Mark did not break forth from the tomb with Jesus. Mark was not returning. Mark was still dead. It was a harsh ending to a week that culminated in resurrection.

I felt that dissonance for many days. Then a deep truth, wrapped up in another sacred ritual, dawned on me: Mark and I have both died. We had been baptized. We had symbolically gone under water, died to ourselves and were raised to life in Christ. This awareness somehow lightened the sadness I was feeling that Easter.

We die first, then we live.

BURNING AND BIRTHING: A NEW YEAR'S RITUAL

Some rituals, like church, hold us in a structure already established. Other rituals are waiting to be created with the communities and structures we desire. In times of grief, so many deep feelings began bubbling up to the surface. Feelings of sadness, hurt, anger and disappointment, I've discovered, can either be forcefully held at bay or lovingly held and honored in ritual. A few years ago, Laura and I created one such ritual.

The last New Year's Eve before Mark died, we were not much into celebrating. We were more than ready to leave the last year behind and hoped beyond hope that the coming year would bring some new life, though we knew that realistically it would bring us our most devastating loss. Laura and I decided to have a Burning and Birthing Celebration. Joe, the kids and I drove over to Mark and Laura's along with a few of their closest friends. Mark was able to enjoy some good food, drink and conversation but tired early and went home to Mom and Dad's house, where he was living for the last year of his life.

After saying our goodbyes to Mark, Laura passed out pieces of paper and instructed everyone to write down something from the year that we wanted to go up in flames. She then instructed us to throw them into the fire.

With a few additional prompts, people began obediently and rather politely writing something on the paper and placing it in the fire, then quickly helping themselves to another appetizer. Laura and I sat madly scribbling away one experience after another that we wanted to see destroyed by fire: hospital visits, emergency meetings, impossible decisions, debt. Joe added quite a few of his own.

"Are you sure no one has anything else they want to violently bid goodbye to from this past year?" Laura asked. No response.

Then the kids asked if they could join. "Sure," we responded. Of course their main interest was throwing things into the fire, but we explained it to them all the same and even helped the three-year-old make a few squiggly lines and toss it carefully into the flames.

Laura and I did a quick reassessment. Hmmm, we thought our burning ritual would be popular with people, knowing how many painful experiences we had been through together. Our next idea was even more "out there," so Laura and I decided to call Bobby. Bobby was one of Mark's best friends and had recently gone through the horror of losing his sister, his only sibling, to a drunk driver. Bobby is a creative and thoughtful soul who understands the importance of ritual, particularly when coupled with deep meaning and alcohol. We needed to be together this night, but he lived four hours away and was unable to make the drive. We told him our plan, which he loved, as we knew he would.

Laura announced like a perfect hostess that we were going out to the garage. "You are welcome to join us for a primal woman-in-labor scream as we symbolically birth in the New Year," she explained, mostly in order to warn people not to call the police. There were a couple awkward smiles from the adults, giggles and excited, confused expressions from the kids. As Laura and I headed for the garage, a little trail of children waddled behind us.

We warned them it would be very loud but not to worry. This would be a kind of get-it-all-out crazy scream, which is good to do from time to time. Then we called Bobby, pulled out Mark's punk rock Hüsker Dü CD, played a particularly cacophonous song at full volume, knowing we could only get away with this on New Year's Eve, and screamed at the top of our lungs, gasped in more breath and kept right on screaming. Pretty soon the door cracked open and Scott, who was having a hard time losing Mark—his mountain climbing, soul-sharing, intellectually stimulating, dear friend—joined us in our primal display of emotion.

"This really helped," Bobby told us over the phone.

I think it helped us all.

PRAYER PRACTICE: *Healing Rituals*

There are endless rituals to either discover or create. Rituals are containers allowing emotions and experiences to be held and engaged creatively. Joe and I have participated in a Shabbat meal with friends at sundown on whatever Fridays we are able to gather. This ritual held us together during the seven difficult years our friends were waiting for their baby to come from China. As we would bless the children among us, we would raise our hands to the East to bless their baby. Now we put our hands on her head, feeling the soft hair under our touch with deep gratitude.

Listen to what kind of ritual you desire to create or find. Ask yourself what needs to be honored right now. Are there emotions or experiences that want to be expressed in a safe, contained environment? Who do you desire to be a part of this ritual?

A ritual can be as simple as offering a toast or telling stories about someone no longer here. A ritual of moving could incorporate bringing dirt or a plant from the former home and planting it at the new home, then having friends journey from room to room praying over the new space, blessing it with their presence.

Engage. Create and engage in your ritual. This might be a one-time thing or a repeated occurrence.

Connect. Rituals often incorporate community. Allow others to honor your journey by inviting them to be a part of your ritual. Connect with God and yourself as you tend to your heart while allowing the larger reality of God and community to hold you.

- twenty-two -

Getting Up Again

When I fall, I shall rise.

MICAH 7:8

WHEN MY DAUGHTER WAS FOUR, she fell at church. This would not be so unusual except that she was carrying the full offering plate to the pastor's waiting hands. She had been ushering for two years, trained by the best, LaDonna and Randy the Mechanic. The congregation gasped, but Allena, being the professional that she was, pulled herself up, gathered the fallen offering and proceeded to dramatically brush herself off, as if she had fallen on filthy ground instead of spotless carpet. After completing her journey, she returned to LaDonna waiting at the back of our small church and loudly retold then reenacted the entire scene that had just unfolded in front of everyone's eyes, including diving on the carpet again and brushing herself off. Allena, at four, was not embarrassed when she fell. She was proud of her ability to get up again.

We all fall down, be it physically, emotionally, spiritually, relationally or financially. Regardless of how or why we've fallen, our physical bodies play an important role in getting up again.

One of my closest friends, Joelle, a therapist who works in the field of addiction recovery and child trauma, understands this. She will often quote to me the Alcoholics Anonymous saying "Move a muscle, change a thought."

Those who have experienced loss are often left confused, unable to figure things out. How do we "change a thought," particularly in times of distress? Our brain chatter can become debilitating, telling us what we did wrong, hinting that we deserved the situation, and spewing judgments every which way. That's what our left brain does in times of stress—it tries to make sense of things and regain control by judging the situation. Unfortunately, many of us have accidentally substituted our left brain's bossiness for the very voice of God.

Sometimes what we need to do is put our colicky brain to bed. One of the best ways I know to do this is to "move a muscle." For me, this often involves surfing or taking a long walk in nature. Before arthritis settled in, I used to run until I was exhausted and didn't have the energy to think those dumb thoughts anymore.

"Move a muscle, change a thought." Thanks, Joelle. Thanks, Alcoholics Anonymous.

WORKING OUT THE GRIEF

Grief is physical. Our bodies hold our trauma and unresolved grief and try to tell us when something is not quite right. Grief can manifest itself physically in any number of ways: tightness of muscles, stomach upset, lack of energy, unexplained pains, headaches, an underlying feeling of being ill at ease. It can feel like we have a cold coming on, a cold that never quite arrives.

There are plenty of physical practices to help work out our grief. Massage can help us notice the places we hold tension and trauma in our bodies and be a gentle means of invoking the self-compassion needed to grieve. A warm bath has become a meaningful practice for me, particularly when I'm feeling overwhelmed or exhausted.

About a year ago, Joe took one of the kids' bathtub crayons and drew a skull and crossbones with the words "Mommy's Bath: Keep Out!" marked boldly on the tile above the tub. I've yet to clean it off.

Yoga is another physical practice that has helped me acknowledge and work with areas of pain. In yoga, I stretch and notice where there is tension in my body. Then I hold the pose and breathe into that tight place until the muscle releases the tension. This is exactly what I am trying to do in grief. I am learning to become aware of the places of pain within me, and instead of ignoring them or quickly moving to the next thing, I am trying to stay with them, to breathe and feel the breath of God enter into the tight places until they release their hold and the trapped energy is transformed into something useful.

When my son was just learning how to walk, he pulled a heavy mirror on top of himself. For a few moments he was trapped under its weight, completely helpless. Akian was physically unharmed, but he was startled and afraid.

I turned to Joelle for advice. She said that when children experience trauma, they feel powerless, and these feelings can get trapped within their bodies. She went on to give me some ways to help our little boy. We had him lay underneath a big suitcase and use his own muscles to lift it off. "Oh no, you're trapped," we'd say, giving him the cue to throw off the suitcase and laugh at his parents' surprised expressions at his incredible display of strength. We did this again and again in hopes that his little muscles would remember how it feels to get untrapped, to regain power, to be able to get up again.

As kids, Mark and I were glued to the TV when watching Mutual of Omaha's *Wild Kingdom*. We especially loved the chase scenes where a deer is chased by a lion but gets away. When this happens in the animal kingdom, once safe the animal often shakes, a physical response to the built-up adrenaline. My friend Jeannie, a therapist trained in Somatic Experiencing, explains that humans need to do the same thing after trauma.

We need to shake. Instead, we often disregard our bodies and keep the trauma trapped inside. We say, "I'm fine," when our bodies are very much not fine. So many of us have been in situations where we could not protect ourselves and no one protected us. These traumas become deeply embedded in our bodies and can be easily triggered; we can become either hyper-alert or disconnected from physical cues. All loss affects our bodies. So what do we do with all the stuff that has built up inside of us? In the movie *Forrest Gump*, the title character takes off running after Jenny, his love, leaves him. He runs for more than three years.

"I just felt like running," he says.

RUNNING WITH THE BULLS

Running with the bulls in Pamplona, Spain, has everything to do with the physicality of grief. (Who knew?!)

When my brother and I, with our spouses, decided to go on the pilgrimage of Santiago de Compostela, I was planning to run with the bulls in Pamplona. Mark had scheduled our trip to coincide with the annual Pamplona festival of Saint Fermin and encouraged me to run with him, something few women do.

When the onset of arthritis began a few weeks before our flight to Spain, leaving me unable to walk or stand without pain, I knew our sibling running plans were over. I sat in a wheelchair touring the Prado Museum in Madrid three days before we were to begin our twenty-one-day journey. Joe is brilliant in solving difficult situations—a happy contribution of his ADHD mind—so we decided that I would attempt to bicycle that first day, and when my knees became too painful, Joe would find a way for me to get to the next town.

That night in Pamplona, we waited anxiously for dawn to break and Mark to enter the barricaded streets, purposely trapping him in the narrow corridor with bulls, and I anxiously waited to find out what my body would do. We slept minimally and uncomfortably between passed-out partiers on a couple of crowded benches. Finally, light crept into the sky, relieving us of the night's misery and getting on with the agenda of the day: bull running and bike riding. To my great surprise, just as Mark began to make his way down to where the runners were lining up, Joe—not exactly a run-with-the-bulls type (or a run-for-any-reason type)—decided to join him.

After a few minutes of frantically running as fast as they could, Mark and Joe plastered themselves against the nearest wall as the bulls appeared and ran right past them. They both made it through safely and without incident, proud to tell the tale. But there is more to it than the masculine bravado of bull running or the drunken partying that coincides with this event. There is something much more significant, historically hidden, mostly forgotten, at the root of this frenetic festival.

This festival of Saint Fermin, at its very core, is a story about the way a community has chosen physically and symbolically to move from places of death to places of life. As with stories of many saints, the historic facts are a little fuzzy. St. Fermin, the patron saint of Pamplona, is believed to have converted to Christianity in the third century. His martyrdom, which was possibly experienced by St. Saturninus but attributed to St. Fermin, resulted from being tied to a bull by his feet and dragged to his death. This martyrdom is at the core of the festival celebrated since 1592.

During the festival, hundreds of people run ahead of the bulls, symbolically enabling St. Fermin to get up again. His murderers did not have the final say. This reenactment plays out the life-death-life story at the core of Christian belief: death is never the end of the story; it comes in the middle.

I watched in disbelief as Joe began to head down to the barricaded alley to join my brother, and I asked him what he was doing.

"I'm running for you," he said.

Joe ran ahead of the half-ton beasts, bringing courage and helping me get up again, and, miraculously, in spite of my arthritis, I was able to pedal all five hundred miles to Santiago.

There are many ways to engage our bodies physically that help us get up again after a loss has knocked us down. When Jews sit shiva, they are allowed to sit in a cocoon of grief surrounded by friends who bring food and comfort. The mourner might very well want to crawl in bed or numb out on TV alone, but there he or she is in deep grief with a house full of people milling around, surrounded by life in a time in which they feel only death. On the last day of shiva, the friends escort the bereaved, as Lauren Winner explains in *Mudhouse Sabbath,* "holding his arm or inching along his side, out the driveway and down the street and around the block, a symbolic (but not merely symbolic) reentry into society."

We often do not want to or feel like moving our bodies, but with the help and encouragement of others, we can find the strength to put one foot underneath us and then the other until we are on our feet again and walking, or running, down the street and around the block.

PRAYER PRACTICE: *Shaking*

Listen to your body. Where do you hold grief? Are there places of trauma that need to be acknowledged and released? How is your body inviting you to "shake"?

Engage by setting aside some time in a quiet, safe space. Lying on your bed, the couch or the floor is usually a good place to begin the process of allowing your body to shake. Begin by shaking your belly, similar to laughing. Many people believe emotions are held in the core of the body and that shaking may release some of them. Let them come up. As you continue to shake, allow the trapped energy of the trauma and grief to release from your body. You may want to shake your arms, hands, legs and feet. Let your body lead the way to what parts need shaking.

Connect with God through honoring the body God has created to house and carry you through this world. Allow God to touch the places of trauma and grief deep within.

Find the ways that allow your body to "shake out" trapped pain. Other suggestions: going for a long run, getting a massage, taking a kickboxing class, hitting a punching bag or pillow.

- twenty-three -

Letting Go

*For a soul will never grow until it is able to
let go of the tight grasp it has on God.*

JOHN OF THE CROSS

I LIKE THE CONCEPT OF LETTING GO about as much as I like the color gray. Yet holding onto grudges, expectations, hurts, people and even my tightly held understandings of God creates a repeated cycle of stagnancy and disappointment. The comforts of clinging and the empowerment of protecting my heart do not satisfy my deepest yearnings for connection. Forgiveness and release seem key. I long to look forward and not back, no longer married to my memories and missing the touch of today. So, I am trying to learn how to forgive Joe for the ways he has hurt me and to let go of unhelpful expectations so that I might be able to see and ask forgiveness for the ways I have hurt him.

I continue to work on forgiving Mark's surgeon for not returning calls or advising us what to do when Mark's brain was herniating and the Emergency Room staff for moving way too slowly and catching it too late.

I also need to forgive myself for not meeting my own expectations and the expectations of others. I recognize my need to let go of the belief that I could have stopped Mark's brain from herniating or should have been able to stop the painful hemorrhaging of our business and finances.

At times I've needed to forgive God for allowing atrocities to tear into my life and the lives of those I love. For being silent in times of great need. For not giving me what I believed I needed in times of scarcity.

Forgiveness, I'm learning, has nothing to do with condoning hurtful behaviors. It is not a means of minimizing harm done or allowing for continued suffering. It does not necessarily mean restoration, which might or might not happen depending on the circumstances.

Forgiveness means no longer putting myself in the judgment seat over another, or over the circumstances of my life, but releasing the wrongdoing to the care and judgment of God. *The Grief Recovery Handbook* defines forgiveness as "giving up the hope of a different or better yesterday." I release the person or situation from my anger and resentment as best I can, allowing God to carry these things. I wash my hands of the offense, or at least that's what I'm trying to learn how to do. Forgiveness is not a magical incantation but a journey of letting go.

I am much better at holding grudges than forgiving. So I am trying to cling to Christ who said, "Forgive them, for they know not what they do" while experiencing tremendous suffering at the hands of people who seemed to know exactly what they were doing.

Slowly, I am learning to say, yes, this happened and I accept this as reality. The deepest engagement of grief, I'm finding, is when I surrender, I forgive, I let go of the things I wish for and want to control, and I accept things as they are. I do not need to judge or make grand proclamations: "This thing that happened was bad, wrong, of the devil, well-deserved or a blessing in disguise, God's will." I can simply say, "This thing has happened, God is here, and I choose to be here too." Even though being here means hurting and longing and being sad, angry and confused sometimes. Being here also means I am choosing to say Yes to life.

SURRENDER AND ACCEPTANCE

The Rule of St. Benedict teaches monks to "day by day remind yourself that you are going to die." When I asked a monk if he thought this was depressing, he responded, "Not compared to the thought that this life is all there is."

Monks practice keeping death close by as a reminder of their humanity. I've read historic accounts of some who have kept a skull on their desk or a grave dug outside their cell. "You are dust, and to dust you shall return," this is the ultimate letting go. Both humility and humanity come from the Latin word *humus*, meaning earth and ground. To be humble is to be grounded in our true humanity. Humility means recognizing and living within our human limitations. These limitations push us into wholeness through dependency on a divine Creator and the help of other people.

Part of accepting the realities of my human limitations is to recognize the importance of surrender. I get stuck in my processes of growth because of my tiny little problem of control. How can I take my clingy hands off the steering wheel? In my favorite book about prayer, *With Open Hands,* Henri Nouwen describes prayer as the process of letting go and surrendering the fears we hold in our tightly clenched fists, allowing our hands to open and receive. This is where trust comes in. If I don't trust or know in some part of my being that there is a greater Presence loving and sustaining this world, then it will be very hard to pry my fingers off my desperate attempts to constantly be in the driver's seat.

People in twelve-step programs are very familiar with the Serenity Prayer penned by theologian Reinhold Niebuhr. I hope to live into this prayer throughout my life: "God, grant me the serenity to accept the things I cannot change; courage to change the things I can; and wisdom to know the difference."

It goes on to say, "Accepting hardships as the pathway to peace."

I remember Allena's first Ash Wednesday service. Many in the church were so excited when she finally came after waiting with us for six long years. I'm pretty sure the older Lutheran ladies basically "prayed her into existence." And here we were carrying this tiny baby up to the front of the church where Pastor Wilk smeared her forehead with ashes and reminded us that we all had to let her go. She too will return to the earth some day. It was a shocking and profound image for me.

Four years later I wanted to bring Mark to the Ash Wednesday service that would have been his last. He was unable to make the trip. As I walked to the front of the church to receive my ashes, I received them for him. "From dust you came, and to dust you shall return."

Sometimes we are forced to let go of things we should never have to let go of.

INTO YOUR HANDS

When Mark took his final breath, the family was there, holding him, holding each other.

It was 7:31 in the morning. I asked if I could sit with his body alone for a few minutes. As I sat beside my brother, I began to recite the daily office of Morning Prayer I pray from my smartphone. We said the prayers together in this sacred space, me very present, unable to be anywhere else but in the strangeness and overwhelming loss of the moment, and Mark gone now on some unknown journey where I could not follow.

Throughout Mark's last two weeks, when he was bedfast and no longer able to communicate, I would talk to him about the mountains he would climb in heaven, *sin ropa*, if he so desired. As it got closer to the end, I'd whisper, "I think this is the hard part of the climb, Mark. Keep going."

Once I walked into the room and heard my dad, unaware of my use of this metaphor, say, "Son, soon you will be exploring mountains in heaven." The morning Mark died, Psalm 24 was the psalm of Morning Prayer that appeared on my phone for that day. Glancing at the passage, holding Mark's lifeless hand, I sat for a moment in stunned appreciation, then began to recite: "Who may climb the mountain of the Lord? Who may stand in his holy place?"

Yes, I breathed in the divine confirmation, Mark is really climbing now.

How do we let go of someone so deeply intertwined in the DNA of our daily lives? And is death really the end? Do we let go of the person completely? In some ways yes, absolutely, undeniably yes. Death is the end.

Mark's wife will not wake up next to her husband anymore. His boys will not hear his voice reading them *Tintin* or feel his arms hoisting them onto another statue. We will not take the trip he had promised me, exploring the painted caves of Baja, the ones you can only get to by mule, and I can't ask him the endless questions that pop into my head that he alone would know the answers to.

But also, no, death is not the end.

Henri Nouwen tells a story of twins arguing with each other in their mother's womb about life after birth. One believes there must be, sensing the squeezes are there to ready them for another place, "much more beautiful than this, where we will see our mother face-to-face." The other twin thinks this is ridiculous, believing this dark and cozy place is all there is. "You have never seen a mother," he rails. "Who put that idea in your head?" Nouwen summarizes the story by saying, "We can live as if this life were all we had . . . or trust that death is the painful but blessed passage that will bring us face-to-face with our God."

Sometimes we are required to open up our hands and let go of things we can't live without. Sometimes all we can do is say, "Into your hands, we commend our spirit" or our brother or our health or our marriage or our children and hope that God's hands are big enough to hold whatever it is that we are unable to hold anymore.

"Into your hands, we commend our spirit."

PRAYER PRACTICE: *The Parting*

Envision yourself on your deathbed. You are taking leave of your body.

Listen to your body and allow your breathing to slow.

Engage. As you are preparing to take mental leave of your body, fill each part with gratitude and love. Start with your hands. Look at them and ponder what they have meant to you. "I am grateful for these hands that have allowed me to work and touch my loved ones, to play the piano, to serve and paint and feel the earth . . ." Then do the same thing for other parts of your body.

Connect with God as you practice letting go with loving appreciation of the body God has given you to journey in from infancy to death.

- twenty-four -

Traveling Companions

The secret of living well is not in having all the answers but in pursuing unanswerable questions in good company.

RACHEL NAOMI REMEN

WHEN MY SON AKIAN WAS THREE, he decided that, in our bedtime routine, he would be the "pointer." After Joe finished telling stories, Allena, then five, would run down the hallway yelling for me to come to our bedroom for prayer time. This was my son's cue to position himself in the hallway, crouch low and point the way for me. He took this role very seriously, sometimes using the fingers on both hands to direct my way, especially when I seemed slightly unsure about the location of my bedroom.

We all need people—traveling companions and pointers—to help us find our way home.

A traveling companion is someone willing to sit in the darkness with us, right in the middle of those excruciating "unanswerable whys." Someone who has developed ways to be present and compassionate with her own dark places. Someone who is willing to suffer with us.

Compassion mirrored through another person awakens compassion in ourselves, and compassion always moves us to better places. It is a trustworthy pointer directing us toward home and healing.

Not everyone, of course, is able to mirror compassion. Sometimes people say things like, "Just give it to God" and run for the nearest door. Or they offer the perfect book, Bible verse, diet or guru-therapist they are sure will fix the problem. Some offer explanations, such as, "It must have been his time to go." Or "This will make you a stronger person." Or "God will use this for good." None of these statements were helpful to me in the aftermath of losing my brother or in facing other disappointments and loss. As it turns out, pain is, well, painful for us and for those trying to comfort us. I try to remember this when people say unhelpful things.

Human relationships are vulnerable, and vulnerability is scary, particularly if we have been deeply hurt or have been previously mistreated. But I am learning that connecting with others is a non-negotiable if I want grief to heal and be transformed. I need to start slowly. I take my cues from the Hokey Pokey: I put my right foot in, then I take it out. I put it back in and shake it all about.

The truth is, there is no substitute for human presence, and that's what it's *really* all about.

HOLDING HANDS

My sister-in-law Laura and I often say we're "holding hands on the downhill." As we were careening down the frightening rollercoaster ride of Mark's illness, we sometimes literally held hands, but more often we used this phrase to feel the other's support emotionally.

Texting has become an incredible means of hand holding for me.

I text my friend Lisa when I'm careening downhill. "Need prayer." Sometimes I add, "Feeling down today," or "Heading into a difficult appointment." No further explanation is necessary. Texting works well in part because it is immediate.

She will often shoot back, "I'm with you."

Texting is also a helpful way to connect because it only requires a few words. In times of need, I rarely want to explain myself or have a conversation. It is amazing how human presence, even in the form of a text, has given me the courage needed to face a difficult situation.

During Mark's illness and death, statements and gentle directives were more helpful than open-ended questions. If someone would say, "How I can help you?" I wouldn't know how to respond. However, if someone said, "I'm coming Wednesday at noon to watch the kids, okay?" I would often gratefully accept the offer. Marilyn, Laura's sister, sometimes came to visit—she'd rent a room at a hotel with a pool and invite us to join her there. Laura and I would drop into the hot tub and watch our kids play as though life were normal. Her boys got to be boys, and it was a needed reprieve from the reality of losing their dad. Laura and I would not have thought to do this ourselves, but those trips to hotel pools were exactly what we needed.

When Mark died, the most helpful things my friends said were comments such as

"I am so sorry your brother died."
"I loved your brother, and I love you."
"Let me tell you a story about your brother."
"Will you tell me stories about your brother?"
"I will not forget your brother."
"I made you some food."
"Tell me if you want me to go away. You will not offend me."

Or they hugged me and took me surfing.

My pastor's wife, Dagmar, said one of my favorite things during this time. She pulled me aside at a church gathering, looked me in the eyes and said in her thick German accent, "Can you believe how much life can give you? Don't you just want to stand in the corner and scream?"

This was exactly what I wanted to do. She was not trying to make me feel better, but instead she gave me permission to feel what I was feeling.

Another immensely helpful comment came after Laura had described some of the unsolvable, excruciating circumstances surrounding Mark's illness and care to her counselor. "This is just completely unacceptable," he responded in his lovely British accent. He then added, "And I think we should all pretend it's not happening."

We all, of course, knew that this was not an option, but his words gave us a little retreat from the dark reality, helped us breathe and even made us laugh. We'd often say this to each other during an impossible situation, mimicking his accent and bringing laughter to each other amidst great pain.

GOOD COMPANY

For many years I have journeyed deeply with three traveling companions on a monthly basis. We are all quite different, including our ages—which vary by thirty years. At one point, we each represented four different decades. We abide by the rules of any meaningful small group:

1. Listen and honor each other's journeys.

2. Share honestly about the state of our hearts and lives. (Sharing struggles is different than gossiping or bitterly complaining about our spouses.)

3. Don't give unsolicited advice.

4. Apologize and try to listen better when we accidentally give unsolicited advice.

5. Eat good food.

6. Trust that something greater than ourselves holds the messy incompleteness of it all. (This helps us not have to fix, solve or give unsolicited advice.)

7. Drink good drink.

8. Honor confidentiality.

9. Do fun and silly things from time to time.

10. Hold hope or faith or joy for one another when needed.

We've supported each other through births and struggles with our children, marriage and divorce, death of a spouse and sibling, spiritual crisis and new faith journeys, and numerous other joys and losses. We've laughed, cried, sat in silence and talked our heads off.

This is the group who helped me discern whether I could write a book while being the present kind of mom I longed to be with two young children.

This is the group who, after Mark died, created a prayer shawl for me. They gathered strips of cloth that held great meaning for them and asked me to bring strips from one of Mark's T-shirts. Chris patiently taught us how to weave on her beautiful wooden loom as Angela, Kristen and I tried hard to listen. We sat around the loom, drinking wine, sharing stories and weaving our love and prayers into the shawl that sits on my nightstand, under a picture of my brother and me, quietly reminding me of the love and prayers of friends.

Discovering Our Great Cloud of Witnesses

My "great cloud of witnesses" on earth have included parents, friends, spiritual directors, therapists, my husband, my faith community, a dead deer in the Maryland woods, the belugas at the aquarium and a group of monks in a California desert, all offering me their presence *with and without words*—mostly without—in the exact times I needed them.

At times I've had to step out of my comfort zone to find what I needed. One such time was while attending a charity event. I found myself seated next to Dr. Ellen Beck, a well-known doctor who works with the homeless and underserved in downtown San Diego. I was drawn to her presence and knew she had wisdom that I longed to tap into.

I can't ask her for her time, she doesn't even know me! I told myself, then heard my voice blurt out, "Will you be my rabbi?"

A ridiculous thing to say, given she is Jewish, yes, but not a rabbi. She did not look surprised but, instead, turned her chair toward mine, took my hand in hers, looked deeply into my eyes and said, "What is it I can do for you?" She then gave me her cell phone number and invited me to come to her home. We have met twice over the past two years and our conversations were exactly what I needed, bringing hope and healing. I'm so glad I had the audacity to ask.

Many of my traveling companions have come through words on paper, from authors in both heaven and on earth. Benedict of Nursia, Anne Lamott, C. S. Lewis, Dr. Seuss, Julian of Norwich, Thomas Merton, J. D. Salinger, Mother Teresa, and my favorite gospel story, *I Love You, Stinky Face*, are a few of my most cherished witnesses.

Others companion me from places beyond this earth. Great Aunt Olive, Jim Young and Mike Yaconelli whisper words of wisdom and courage. Mark has joined this "great cloud of witnesses" of course, mischievously covering me in a deeper mystery, both further away then I ever wanted to endure and ever present in ways that have surprised me.

I have been grateful for so many who have helped me open back up to life when an event knocked the life out of me. Asking for help is not the easiest thing to do, but the alternative is usually much harder. When things are not well with our hearts, souls and circumstances, wisdom moves us to search for help. Finding a therapist, spiritual director or a twelve-step group, pursuing the right medications, joining a meaningful small group, finding an exercise partner are a few of the endless resources available to help us transform the pain into something useful and life-giving.

Pride says, "I can do it on my own."

Wisdom says, "Find the help you need."

Sometimes we "come to that place in life where we know all the words but none of the music," as Sue Monk Kidd did in her forties. During a time when I couldn't hear the music of hope, my friend Gayle had me write "hope" on a napkin and give it to her. "I will hold this for you as long as you need me to," she said.

Sometimes I have been the paraplegic found in Mark 2, unable to carry my mat or my faith or hope or joy or responsibilities. This is what community is for. Sometimes we carry—and sometimes we are carried—to the places we need to go. My traveling companions carried me through the darker days, becoming my hope, that "thing with feathers," poet Emily Dickinson writes about, "that perches in the soul and sings the tune without the words, and never stops at all."

THE LOVE CIRCLE

Every year on Christmas Eve my whole family gathered around the glass table in my folks' living room for the "Love Circle." On the table was a candleholder made by an elderly gentleman from my childhood church. Mom would prop a decorative poinsettia against its side. The lights were dimmed and Mark would light the Advent candle. This was Mark's job each year, starting when we were very young. Then Dad would read the passage from John: "The light shines in the darkness, and the darkness has not overcome it" (John 1:5 ESV).

We prayed together in a circle surrounding the candle, holding hands. We thanked God for this circle of family, for our health, for how our lives had unfolded the past year.

Four months after Mark had gone we sat in this love circle, missing him terribly. We sat in awkward silence, gathered around the same candleholder and poinsettia, sadly aware of our circle's incompleteness.

Then his eleven-year-old son slowly lifted the wooden pole that brings the candle up out of its glass encasing and set the wick aflame. We paused to take it in. Dad cleared his throat and began to read: "The light shines in the darkness, and the darkness has not overcome it."

Somehow, in the midst of these broken and beautiful people, performing this ritual, hearing these words, watching this tiny flame illuminate our tears and shadow dance on the wall behind us, I knew it was true.

PRAYER PRACTICE: *Intentional Conversation*

Grief, as we know, often feels like being held under water. Sometimes what we need is to buddy breathe. Buddy breathing happens when a scuba diver loses his or her air supply and another diver comes alongside and shares air, allowing both to breathe until they surface. I've done a lot of buddy breathing through my journeys of grief. My traveling companions have all shared their oxygen with me when I've lost mine.

When scuba divers lose air, they will do anything to find some. They don't politely wait until another scuba diver passes by and asks if they need help. They wave their arms and give the distress signal. We should learn from this. When we can't breathe, we should wave wildly and ask for help.

Listen. Ask God to help you connect with people to journey through times of loss.

Engage. Make requests of others, even if it feels uncomfortable or humbling. Sometimes even your closest friends may not realize exactly what the loss is doing to you. Tell them. If you think counseling or a twelve-step group will help, try it. Keep seeking and asking until you find the right person, or people, to journey with you. Your heart will know who the right people are, and relief will come.

Connect on a regular basis with another person or group of people. There is no substitute for human presence, particularly in the isolating journey of grief.

Sometimes our traveling companions in times of grief are not the people we expect them to be (best friend, pastor, spouse). That is why it is important to look beyond our expectations to find who God is providing as a companion.

twenty-five

Learning to Float

Grief makes you stupid.

MY SISTER-IN-LAW SARA

WHEN SURFING IN BAJA, I once made the mistake of paddling out at San Miguel, known for its healthy population of sea urchins, without booties. Needless to say, I made quite a sacrifice of my tender feet in order to surf that day. When I got home I gave my feet the attention they required. I cleaned the wounds, slapped on some ointment and Band-Aids, and walked as gingerly as possible for the next few days. I am pretty good at recognizing physical wounds, treating them tenderly and helping them heal. When it comes to emotional wounds, however, I am not the sharpest pencil in the box, though the needs and care required are similar.

I'm trying to learn to tread lightly. I can't always wear booties to protect myself from the barbs of life, but I can offer tenderness to my wounded parts. I can recognize my injuries, whether they are physical or emotional, and I can cut myself a little slack and give myself the necessary gentleness and attention needed to heal.

I grew up believing others' needs were more important than my own. I've come to recognize this as a formula for burnout. The source of love, it turns out, is bottomless, so I can extravagantly love my neighbors, myself, my God and have enough left over to "love" my favorite beverage or animal or sports teams if I so desire. At times, I've been forced to admit that focusing outward can be easier and serve as a distraction so I don't have to address the internal needs. The remark "It is better to give than receive. It is also easier," attributed to Vincent de Paul, hits home.

SELF-COMPASSION

The need for self-compassion and practical self-care is heightened in times of grief. I do need to place the oxygen mask on myself before I help my children or others, as the flight attendants instruct. If I can't breathe, I can't help others breathe. Self-compassion means developing healthy means of self-care. This includes rest, exercise, eating well, connecting with friends and doing things I love.

Grief, I've found, takes energy and is unpredictable; it ebbs and flows. It cares nothing for my schedules or priorities—nor if I floss regularly. When I grieve, my body is working hard simply to function, and I'm learning that grief is a time to do less. I have adapted G. K. Chesterton's quote as a mantra: "If a thing is worth doing, it is worth doing badly." To me this means that although I still need to feed my children, a plate of microwaved chicken nuggets with some carrot sticks thrown on is okay sometimes.

Grief can be a forced retreat, pulling me off the frontlines in order to tend to my wounded parts, to reassess, reorganize and realign my life around what is truly important to me. Learning to love myself means noticing when weariness is creating parched wastelands in my internal landscape and seeking the help I need to get to water.

One form of self-care that is particularly needed in times of grief is the ability to self-soothe. When children are not able to develop skills to calm themselves in times of distress, they become clingy and overly dependent on others, usually a parent. When adults are unable to self-soothe, we do the same thing. We cling to any number of powerful choices available to numb the internal chaos or find others to be our security blanket. This, of course, is not the healthiest foundation for relationships. The problem is, the "security blanket" friend inevitably ends up leaving, and the anesthetizing effects of TV ends when we shut the device off. We are left where we started, in need of comfort.

On September 11, 2001, Joe and I were staying at my folks' house after just moving back to San Diego from Maine. Joe was at work, and I wandered downstairs and found a note scribbled on a sticky note in Dad's handwriting: "horrific news on TV."

I poured some coffee and made my way into the living room. Live before my disbelieving eyes was the second plane smashing into the World Trade Center and the complete chaos that followed. When that second plane hit, it wiped out the possibility of this being an accident, and the whole world knew in that moment that we were under attack. Someone was intentionally flying airplanes full of innocent people into buildings also full of thousands of innocent people. We all remember the day. It changed us, like the assassination of President Kennedy changed the generation before us. Anything can happen. Anyone can be killed, and whole skyscrapers can come down filled with fathers and husbands, wives, sisters and sons—people no one should have to live without.

The first thing I needed to do was be around other people who were talking about these horrors. Everyone I knew was at work. I called Joe, talked for a few minutes, and then when he had to go, I drove to a familiar coffee house and sat among strangers, listening in on bits and pieces of conversations. Then, not knowing what else to do, I went surfing.

This is inappropriate, I thought. *I should be doing something somber.* The ocean, however, is a "thin place" for me, and it has long been a receptacle of grief, a place that welcomes tears. Saltwater returns to saltwater. So off I trudged to my place of comfort where I let my tears flow into the ocean's embrace.

That night the whole country grieved together in front of our television sets. Usually I find that TV watching is a distraction or vacation from grief, but that night it was a means of grieving. Even those of us who didn't know anyone in the towers called loved ones across the country just to hear familiar voices. I was grateful to be hunkered down with my husband, mom and dad, knowing that my brother and sister-in-law were just four short miles away. And New York, a city that had seemed so distant, so hostile just yesterday, was now our neighbor, filled with people who hurt just like us and who were in unbelievable pain.

A few days later, Dan Rather went on *Late Night with David Letterman* and was overcome by the grief his city was experiencing. As he choked back tears, Letterman grabbed his hand and went to a commercial break. The cloud was pierced, the restrictions lifted, and we all cried, held hands and became human for one sacred moment.

Finding ways to grieve meant connecting with others and connecting with myself in self-soothing ways. A coffee house full of strangers, the ocean, carrying a little sticky note with Dad's writing on it around in my pocket, staying glued to the news with family, talking to friends on the phone and watching Dan Rather and David Letterman all helped me grieve and brought me comfort in a frightening and vulnerable time.

CREATING ORDER IN CHAOS

While sitting in the old ranch house at Saint Andrew's Abbey with a group of close friends, the fireplace suddenly began pouring dark smoke into the room. Everyone immediately jumped up and worked to quickly assess the situation. Libbie went straight for the doors to let some air in, Mike poked around in the fireplace attempting to reopen the old metal flue. When that didn't work, Archie and Will carefully removed the burning log, and Jeannie found a fan. I collected all the dirty mugs and rushed them to the sink. Afterward, we had a good laugh at my choice of crisis management. Why was clearing dirty dishes what I decided needed to happen in this moment of chaos? I know why. *Order.* If I can't control the biggies, like the house burning down, I can make sure the kitchen is clean.

I've been doing a lot of kitchen cleaning lately, and sometimes, this really does help. It helps me to have areas in my home I can go to and feel rested because everything is clean, in its proper place, and nothing is calling out to me to fix, sort, clean, organize or tend to it. This is a means of self-care for me.

I daily take my proverbial machete and whack away at the encroaching jungle of email, needs of children, dinner duties and dirty dishes. And the very next day, or sometimes the very next minute, it's all grown back. I don't have the energy to whack away at my husband's piles. Nor can I bring order to my children's toys—items that prefer to be underfoot rather than safely returned to the baskets that are picturesquely tucked under the church pew in our living room. At these moments, I find myself fantasizing about single life. Once upon a time, I would put things in their place and they would stay there, right there, where I left them. It was amazing.

I recognize the calming effect clutter-free environments have on me. My internal landscape is allowed to believe that it too can find simplicity. When I toured a Shaker village or sat in a Buddhist meditation hall, I found myself experiencing a deep sense of peace. My surroundings are important to my body and spirit, so I don't judge this—I only acknowledge it and work to find places of order and beauty, particularly in the internal or external disorder of grief.

I go to the stream, or the coffee house in the old brick building downtown, with just one good book in my bag, or I go to the library and check out Hiroshige's *Sixty-Nine Stations* and lose myself in his

Japanese landscapes, or I go to the monastery where I can be quiet and alone. I rest and breathe and let the beauty, order and simplicity come in through my eyes and affect my body and my mind, giving me energy to return to the sacred clutter of community.

This is what self-care does. It gives us energy to come home to ourselves and return to life. "Grief makes you stupid" in many ways. We misplace things, we get lost in our own neighborhoods, and we forget things like our children's names, what year it is and how to tenderly care for this precious body of ours that has been through so much.

LOVING THE ENEMY WITHIN

"Self-care is never a selfish act," Parker Palmer assures us, "it is simply good stewardship of the only gift I have, the gift I was put on earth to offer to others. Anytime we can listen to true self and give it the care it requires, we do so not only for ourselves but for the many others whose lives we touch." Selfishness, I am beginning to understand, is often the result of not loving and caring for myself properly. I am learning that if I am unable to love myself well, I will not be able to love others well. I will "love" them out of my places of brokenness and need. I will act in "loving" ways toward my neighbor and all the while harbor resentment and feelings of irritation or self-righteousness.

So, I try to begin my day by asking, "God, how do you desire to be with me today?" and "How do you desire for me to be with you?" These simple prayers open my awareness to the myriad ways God pours out blessings and love on me. They allow me to respond in kind, acknowledging that God knows what I need even more than I do. This opens up compassion in me that I believe comes from God and flows both into and through me.

I have often wrestled with the passage "Love thy enemies." I would rack my brain trying to come up with an enemy. Then it dawned on me that this includes my enemies within. I have no problem coming up with the parts of myself I am at enmity with. Judgmentalism and rigidity are two of my sharp corners that make me cringe; yet instead of pretending they are not there, I have begun to offer compassion to these parts of me. When I do this, their power is immediately diffused; they become less scary and less damaging to me and others. I envision these areas slowly being worn away by the waves of acceptance and compassion.

WAVES OF TRANSFORMATION

Waves of grief that pummel us can also lead us home.

In *The Wizard's Tide,* a story thinly masking Frederick Buechner's childhood experience of losing his father to suicide, the young boy Teddy gets tumbled by a wave. "Don't fight it," his dad tells him. "It's too big to fight. Just let it do what it wants with you. . . . It's even sort of fun being rolled if you just give in to it and don't hit back." Teddy is not so sure. "After all," his father adds, "the wave is just trying to take you where you want to go anyway."

"Where do you mean?" Teddy asks.

"Why, the dry land," his dad responds. "That's where waves go. Home, where else?"

A couple of years back, I began to notice weathered bricks scattered along the shore where I surf. It struck me as odd that I hadn't noticed them the past twenty years. The bricks have holes bored through them, revealing their initial use as weights for crab and lobster traps, which now make perfect candle holders. What I am drawn to is their corners, once sharp, now worn smooth by the sea. I have them scattered all over my deck, icons of hope, reminders that the relentless wearing down of life can bring deep beauty and soft hearts.

Each time I surf, I now practice floating. It is a prayer practice for me. I hop off my board, lie back, open my arms to the sky and let the ocean hold me. In doing so, I am allowing my body to feel that I am not in control, I don't have to be, and though life can be dangerous, wind-whipped and wave-tossed, there is a reality underneath me that will hold.

> Lie back, daughter, let your head
> be tipped back in the cup of my hand,
> gently, and I will hold you . . .
> and let go, remember,
> when fear cramps your heart,
> what I told you:
> lie gently and wide open to the light-year stars,
> lie back and the sea will hold you.

Pilgrimage is all about leaving home, going on a formational journey and coming home changed. Or, as T. S. Eliot wrote, "And the end of all our exploring will be to arrive where we started and know the place for the first time." This was my experience in the pilgrimage through Spain and even more so as I have traveled through loss. It is through the stripping and surrounding beauty, the failures and the hands that have lifted me up, through going "over the falls" and through floating, through the wearing down and the letting go, that I can now look in the mirror and, for the most part, like very much the face staring back at me. I see the laugh lines along with the scars.

And yes, the righteous indignation, the fear, the judgment and rigidity, I see you in there too, and you are loved.

PRAYER PRACTICE: *Doing What We Love*

In one of my favorite lines in the film *Chariots of Fire*, Eric Liddell says, "I believe that God made me for a purpose. . . . But he also made me fast! And when I run I feel his pleasure."

Surfing is where I feel God's pleasure. The day my Aunt Tootsie handed me a blue and red blow up raft and sent me into the waves changed my life forever. I remember the sheer delight in feeling the wave hurtle me forward, God's pleasure wrapping around my own.

God has wired us for pleasure. We are all created to deeply enjoy life in different ways. Sometimes, of course, we get this all messed up and seek pleasure in unhelpful ways. When we feel God's pleasure because we have found things we love to do, it opens us to God, to ourselves and to others. When we find pleasure in unhealthy ways, it disconnects us from God, ourselves and others. We know the difference.

Doing what we love brings energy needed to do the things that need to get done, be it our everyday duties or tending the darkness within. I am a better Christian when I surf. I am a better wife and mother too. Joe will often say when I'm particularly irritable and negative, "Honey, when's the last time you were in the ocean?" In grief work, it is a very good idea to find what we love and do it, to "follow our bliss," as Joseph Campbell teaches.

Listen. What do you love to do? What brings you life and energy? Think back to childhood. How did you play? What did you love to do then? What do you remember? Did you draw, explore, read, let your mind wander, build things, play games with friends? This might connect you to the place within that is worthy of your time and attention.

Engage. Do something that feeds your spirit. Do things you love to do because they make you happy or peaceful or comforted or creative. Do something that leaves you feeling strong and alive.

Connect. Feel God's pleasure as you find what you love. You'll know you've found it when gratitude is your natural response.

twenty-six

Coming Home to Our Broken Hallelujahs

God is always at home.
It is we who have gone out for a walk.

MEISTER ECKHART

W HEN MY HUSBAND AND I moved to our loft in downtown San Diego's East Village, I embraced everything
about urban life, even the sirens, the three competing rock bands,
the parking problems, the lost tourists, the drunk bar-hoppers and
the homeless people sleeping outside our building.

I embraced everything, I should say, *except* the guys who ran the
tattoo parlor across the street. They scared me. A gang of them would
camp out in a row of chairs out front. They blared obscene music at
two in the morning, got into fights in the middle of the street and
harassed people who passed by. They were the reason I didn't walk
on that side of the street and why I didn't always like coming home.

We were deep in the throes of unsuccessful in vitro fertilization,
our money and my energy greatly depleted with no guarantee offspring would be in our future. I needed my home to be a sanctuary,

a place I could tuck into, return to and feel safe. It felt like the tattoo guys were robbing me of all of that.

For two years, I glared out our third-floor window, sending hate-filled vibes their way. "What are you thinking about?" Joe would ask. Still glaring, I'd answer, "I am fantasizing about shooting out the tires of their big, black trucks." Joe held his tongue from saying, "Beth, it's been over two years. Get over it."

I remember coming home feeling peaceful and centered after a three-day silent retreat at the monastery and, within minutes, I was screaming the worst words I knew out the window at them then dashing behind the curtain so they wouldn't know it was me.

Things were a little tense.

I did not want to listen to their music as I slept, or tried to sleep, and I felt justified in my hatred. I also began to feel slightly convicted about the whole "love thy neighbor" thing.

Then one early afternoon as I was sitting out on our fire escape, staring down at the tattoo guys across the street, I called Joe at work. "Joe, I'm going to get a tattoo. You okay with that?"

He laughed, not sure I was serious.

I had never wanted a tattoo. I was one of the few people in my generation with no body art.

"Yeah, sure," he said distractedly. In less than an hour I called him back and announced, "I did it."

Joe left work early and hurried home. He came through the door with a "Really?" look on his face. I peeled off the plastic protective covering on my left wrist, revealing the delicately scripted words, "Love Thy Neighbor."

I explained how I'd walked to the ATM and withdrawn some cash, then marched across the street, took a deep breath, and stepped through the doorway and into the tattoo parlor. The walls were covered with skulls, bloody knives, naked women and the Virgin of Guadalupe. The proprietor, who I'd later find out was named Chato, was working on somebody's backside. "Excuse me, I'm your neighbor from across the street. May I watch you?" He looked up at me and gave a half nod.

Sitting there in my pink T-shirt and ponytail, I noticed I was the only one in the room without piercings, tattoos or black clothing. After watching Chato a while, I forced myself to step out onto the sidewalk and have a seat in one of the chairs in front of the shop. I tried to relax and take it all in; I studied the world from their perspective. The guy next to me asked what I was getting done.

"Love thy neighbor," I muttered.

"Why?" he asked. *Oh no*, I thought.

"Well, you guys are my neighbors, and I'm having trouble loving you. You kind of scare me," I sputtered. "You know, with the fights that break out over here and all . . ."

"Whoa! That is so cool!" he exclaimed. He hopped up and ushered me back into the shop and announced with complete sincerity, "Chato, dude, we're scaring our neighbors! We gotta stop fighting!"

Chato was not quite so touched by the story.

"Hey," he said defensively, "I'm just tryin' to run my place."

I blurted out that I was not trying to get him to change; I just wanted to get this tattoo.

The tattoo artist next to Chato said, "Love Thy Neighbor? Like with brass knuckles and sh—?"

"No, that's not exactly what I had in mind," I responded.

He found a tattoo magazine and turned to a picture of "Love Thy Neighbor" tattooed on a man's inner forearm—with a bloody knife in the background.

"That's not exactly it, either," I said.

Chato, who I imagined had learned his penmanship behind bars, began to methodically prepare his tools. A few of the tattooed locals gave me a thoughtful rundown on all the care and instructions for a first-timer, and Chato began to do his art on my wrist.

Then he stopped. "How do you spell 'Thy'?" he said shyly, and added, "I didn't go to school."

The other tattoo artist piped in, "Dude, it's not because you didn't go to school, it's because you don't read the Bible! It's all over that book."

After that day, when Joe came home I would often be out on the fire escape waving to my new friends at the tattoo parlor. Joe said the shift in my behavior was jarring. "You hated these guys, wanted to shoot out their tires, and now you're making them cookies?"

Hmm. I'd already forgotten.

After that day, the music that came streaming across the street from the tattoo parlor was not so grating. It seemed like fewer fights broke out. The sidewalk felt safe to me. I'm not sure anything really changed other than my perspective, but I felt at home in my neighborhood.

Joe skeptically joked about whether my "new friends" actually remembered me, if I was even on their radar.

Then about four months later, I took our car in for an oil change at the shop two blocks over. As I entered the office I noticed Chato talking to the repairman behind the counter.

"Excuse me, Chato? Hi, I'm Beth. I'm not sure if you remember me . . ."

Before I could finish, his face broke into a smile, and he stepped forward and gave me a warm hug.

"Hey," he said to his friend behind the counter, "This is my neighbor, the one I was telling you about."

The anger that accompanied grieving the losses involved in our fertility journey pushed me across the street and into my tattoo parlor neighbor's door. That one act did much more than I could have imagined. It caused my heart to grow three sizes that day like the Grinch's and changed my perspective. It also allowed my home to be the sanctuary I longed for, granted with music a little louder than I normally enjoy.

Grief has often separated me from others, leaving me feeling isolated and alone. The tattoo incident permanently etched into my brain—and my arm—the realization that I can push through my resistance and cross streets that are difficult to cross. Hopeless situation can turn into powerful connections and my stubborn heart can change.

I can only hope other journeys of grief in my life will follow suit. We journey within or down or through some unwelcome event alone, and we return changed, ready to return to community and relationships. We do not ride off into the sunset or down into the caverns or across the street never to be seen again; we come home with the gifts of our expanded hearts and transformed presence.

Let it be so.

ALTAR CLOTHS

One bright Sunday morning when Joe and I first moved into the loft across from Chato's tattoo parlor, we walked to church, still deciding if the local Lutheran congregation was to be our home. We arrived to some commotion in the side chapel. The narrow strip of cloth that drapes over the altar had been stolen. Church began as usual, and we thought no more about it until Sheila, a large and mentally ill homeless woman, began to process down the middle aisle. She was wearing bright pink lipstick smeared generously over her lips and well beyond, and donning nothing above the waist but the missing altar cloth.

The pastor continued with his liturgical prayer, as Sheila situated herself in the front row. LaDonna, the usher that morning, subtly offered her some covering that actually covered. She refused. When the choir rose to sing, she too rose, stood in front of the church and began to direct them with a bathroom key attached to a large wooden spoon she had taken and not returned from some unknown location. The choir got much more than they expected that morning as they tried to keep a straight face while Sheila directed them, doing "the dance of the seven veils, with six of them in the wash," to use a favorite expression of my grandmother's.

I loved watching how the pastor and LaDonna showed no signs of anxiety or embarrassment about what was occurring but simply flowed with the situation. But my favorite part of the morning was the liturgical prayer spoken over us at the very moment Sheila walked down the center aisle: "God comes to comfort the disturbed and to disturb the comfortable."

As we walked home, Joe and I knew we had found our church home. We needed this community to expose us to the God who both comforts and disturbs.

I have begun to trust in and come home to a God who might at times disturb me or be hidden within life's disruptions. God's "plan" for me will not necessarily involve smooth sailing from here on out, even if I prayerfully discern my every move and do everything in my ability to follow in Jesus' footsteps. We all know where those footsteps led him. Why am I so surprised when mine, too, lead to places of suffering? I am coming home to a God who is present in my suffering, already in the storm-tossed boat, who at times shatters my complacency and at others envelops me in comfort, kissing my scraped knees and tending to my broken heart.

Mother Teresa described suffering as "a kiss of Jesus." Christians historically and globally have understood that Jesus draws close to those who suffer, intimately close. Maybe when I am very old I will look back on my life and realize that the suffering has been a long, slow kiss of Jesus. Slowly, slowly, yet with the most powerful magic, he is kissing us, drawing us to himself, filing down our egos, softening our brick corners, transforming our hurts into something beautiful, making all things well.

THANKS AND YES

During the past seven years, I have been intimately involved in journeys of birth and death. I have watched the first breaths of my two children and the last breath of my brother. Arrivals and departures are sacred. I have come to believe that we are closest to home in our infancy and in our dying, when we are the most vulnerable and dependent. And we are often the farthest from our true home at the very height of our successes and independence, when, according to the U-bend article in *The Economist* I mentioned earlier, we are also the least happy.

Perhaps the fact that I will most likely begin and end my pilgrimage in this world diminished is by design. Perhaps the brutal letting go of ego, of expectations, of control is not only a part of aging but a preparation for my home going

I am carrying around a piece of Eden that I am meant to carry. Our story begins there, where we were created in the very image of God and called "very good." The fall, I am trying to remember, is not where our story begins. We start this journey at home, we leave, mess things up, get battered by our experiences and discover a God who journeys with us, inviting us always to return home. Sin, cynicism, cancer and the cross all come in the middle. "Grace," as Anne Lamott is fond of saying, "bats last."

Through my journeys of grief, I have come to recognize that Eden is not the hills above my childhood home where my Playmate would wait for me, sending gentle breezes and shining, warm sunlight on my face. Eden is not the time I long to return to, where wounds were magically kissed away by a loving parent. No, these things are reminders of a deeper reality, my home underneath my temporal existence.

"Eden," as Thomas Merton reminds us, "is the heart of Christ," a place always available to me, always present.

Coming home means accepting that God has something different for my life than I had thought. Sometimes we get to see the benevolent workings of a master architect. I got a glimpse of this when the timing of Joe's new job coincided to the day of Mark's death. This helped restore my belief that I can trust in a loving, intimately orchestrating God, even when, so often, I cannot see or feel God's presence.

Sometimes even in the darkness and perceived absence of God, a divine whisper breaks through, like the morning I found out Mark's tumor was rapidly growing back. Allena, then three and having no idea what was going on, woke up that morning, walked into the kitchen and sang, "He's got you and uncle Marco in his hands, he's got you and Aunt Lola (Laura) in his hands." Tears filled my eyes as I felt God's presence, and then she added with a giggle, "He's got you and my potty in his hands . . . He's got the whole world in his hands." Yes, I smiled, feeling God's breath and humor enter into my asthmatic soul. Thanks be to God.

I now know that there is something beyond the happy hallelujah of our childhood or of the childhood we had hoped to have. There is a full, abundant, joy-filled and grief-enriched hallelujah to be found deeply embedded in the very story of our lives.

HALLELUJAH

A few weeks before Mark died, we listened to Rufus Wainwright's version of Leonard Cohen's "Hallelujah," sitting together, holding hands. By that point, Mark's short-term memory had entirely disappeared and he had trouble recognizing his own home—but he began to hum the melody. His hum turned into a mumble. Then, slowly, the words came; he had found them there, inside his disordered brain, and sang along. I fumbled for my smartphone and pressed record, wanting to hold on to the moment forever, his weak, almost inaudible voice singing about love not being a "victory march." I added my voice softly, and together we sang, "It's a cold and it's a broken hallelujah . . ."

Hallelujah, hallelujah, hallelujah, hallelujah.

Grief invites us to stand at the intersection of human and divine, stripped of ourselves, vulnerable to movements of grace. But it takes courage to stand at that corner and recognize the cross before us, etched unexpectedly into the road we are on.

The divine whispers are ever calling. Sometimes I hear them, mostly I don't, but I hear them enough to realize there is an unbroken hallelujah found deep within the fabric of my life.

Hallelujah, hallelujah, hallelujah, hallelujah.

Acknowledgments

Ever Thanks

I am ever grateful for the seed of this book, implanted in my heart on a walk through Mission Trails in San Diego, and for the unfolding of opportunity, discernment and practical wisdom that nurtured this project into being.

My midwives:

Cindy Bunch, my editor, for taking a chance on me and being both tough and tender through the birthing process.

Angela Coriale, Heather Bickel Stevenson, Jeremy Stevenson, Martha Radatz, Wilk Miller, Lisa Wondercheck, Aaron Lawson, Tracy Cambell and Sara Kuljis for shaping, questioning and deepening this book.

Lisa Lehr, gifted in both editing and spiritual direction, for having the audacity to say, "You're staying on the surface here, sounds like you need to push through something."

Jennifer Grant for her generosity with both red pen and kind words.

Kristen Montgomery, Chris Justice and Angela Coriale for listening and playing.

Joelle Tonkovich for her calming presence and for keeping me in the sanctuary of the sea.

Laura Allen for kicking "at the darkness until it bleeds daylight" (to quote a favorite singer-songwriter Bruce Cockburn), for always being a hand hold away, and for photographing me for this book and Mark and me at a favorite spot in Mulege, Baja California, Mexico.

JuliAnn Sands, my sister-in-law, for making me look better than I should in my photo.

Joe, my love and life partner, for unconditionally accepting this project into our lives, and for helping me remember you are not my home, you are my traveling companion, and I am grateful.

Allena and Akian for teaching me everything I need to know about the kingdom of heaven.

My parents, Hollis and Grace Allen, for a lifetime of love, support and stability.

Mark for being proud of his little sister and making me laugh, even now.

Chris Justice, Noel Estergren, Jeannie Oestreicher and Mary Byrne Hoffman, my spiritual directors who have journeyed with me through different parts of my broken hallelujahs.

I can no other answer make but thanks, and thanks, and ever thanks.

Notes

INTRODUCTION

p. 12   One of my favorite songs: Leonard Cohen's song "Halle-
         lujah" was originally recorded on his album *Various Posi-
         tions* (Sony, 1984). The lyrics can be found in *Stranger Music:
         Selected Poems and Songs* (Toronto: McClelland & Stewart,
         1993). The song exploded in popularity through Jeff Buck-
         ley's cover version. Other well-known covers include Rufus
         Wainwright and my favorite, k.d. lang.

CHAPTER 2: LONGING FOR HOME

p. 23   "If I find in myself a desire": C. S. Lewis, *Mere Christianity*
         (New York: Macmillan, 1943), 120.

p. 28   "For Thou hast made us for Thyself": Augustine of Hippo's
         words come to us from the fourth century in *The Confes-
         sions of St. Augustine*, bk. 1.1 (New York: Sheed & Ward,
         1942), 3.

CHAPTER 3: LOVE AND DISILLUSIONMENT

p. 34   "the love that consists in this": Rainer Marie Rilke, *Letters
         to a Young Poet* (New York: Norton, 1963), #7, p. 59.

p. 35   "the most painful act the human being can perform": An-
         thony De Mello writes beautifully about love and the act
         of seeing in *The Way to Love: Meditations for Life* (New
         York: Doubleday, 1992). "The terror that comes to the ro-
         mantic lover when he decides to really see that what he
         loves is not his beloved but his image of her. That is why
         the most painful act a human being can perform, the act
         that he dreads the most is the act of seeing. It is in the act
         of seeing that love is born, or rather more accurately, the
         act of seeing is Love" (98).

CHAPTER 4: LOSING MY STRENGTH

p. 40   "People wish to be settled": Ralph Waldo Emerson, *The Essential Writings of Ralph Waldo Emerson* (New York: Classic Books International, 2010), 167.

CHAPTER 5: LONGING FOR A CHILD

p. 48   "still longing for love": Julian of Norwich, a fourteenth-century English anchoress living in a cell attached to the church of St. Julian in Norwich, England, assures us many times in *Showings* (New York: Paulist Press, 1978) of God's ability to make "all things well" (229). Julian goes on to talk about "secret touchings of sweet spiritual sights and feelings" (ibid., 255).

CHAPTER 6: LOSING MY BROTHER

p. 58   "And even though it all went wrong": From Leonard Cohen's "Hallelujah," originally recorded on his album *Various Positions* (Sony, 1984). The lyrics can be found in *Stranger Music: Selected Poems and Songs* (Toronto: McClelland & Stewart, 1993).

p. 59   "Abba, I belong to you": This is the breath prayer Brennan Manning widely taught and personally used. He writes about it in *The Furious Longing of God* (Colorado Springs: David C. Cook, 2009), 46.

CHAPTER 7: LOSING MY RELIGION

p. 61   "a sound of bolting": From C. S. Lewis's brutally honest book *A Grief Observed* (New York: Seabury, 1961), 9, written after his wife died of cancer.

p. 64   Psalms of Disorientation: Walter Brueggemann's helpful breakdown of the Psalms as "Orientation, Disorientation and New Orientation" is found in *The Message of the Psalms: A Theological Commentary* (Minneapolis: Augsburg, 1984), and the devotional *The Spirituality of the Psalms* (Minneapolis: Augsburg, 2002).

p. 64   "Further up and further in": Well-known words of C. S. Lewis from *The Last Battle* (New York: Collier, 1956), 161.

p. 65   Prayer Practice: Writing a Lament: This prayer practice has been compiled with the help of Walter Brueggemann's work in *The Spirituality of the Psalms* (Minneapolis: Fortress, 2002), and *The Message of the Psalms: A Theological Commentary* (Minneapolis: Augsburg, 1984).

CHAPTER 8: FALLING INTO DEPRESSION

p. 68   "When you stop expecting people to be perfect": Donald Miller's remarks are from *A Million Miles in a Thousand Years* (Nashville: Thomas Nelson, 2009), 206.

p. 71   "Age and Happiness: The U-bend of Life": From *The Economist*, December 18, 2010, 33-36.

p. 72   the necessary shattering of our security structures: Richard Rohr, *Falling Upward: A Spirituality for the Two Halves of Life* (San Francisco: Jossey-Bass, 2011).

p. 72   "Unfortunately, forward thrust turns out not to be helpful": Anne Lamott is the only author I know who can make me burst out laughing while writing touchingly on grief. Her words are from *Stitches: A Handbook on Meaning, Hope and Repair* (New York: Riverhead Books, 2013), 32.

p. 73   "They say the darkest hour is right before the dawn": From Bob Dylan's song "Meet Me in the Morning," *Blood on the Tracks* (Sony, 1975).

CHAPTER 9: MINIMIZING OUR WOUNDS

p. 82   "Save me from my own private, poisonous urge": Thomas Merton's prayer to accept life as it comes is found in *Dialogues with Silence: Prayers and Drawings* (San Francisco: HarperSanFrancisco, 2001), 53.

CHAPTER 10: ACKNOWLEDGING OUR LOSSES

p. 86   "like a person who clears his throat": Quoted in Belden Lane's *The Solace of Fierce Landscapes: Exploring Desert and Mountain Spirituality* (New York: Oxford University Press, 1998), 179.

CHAPTER 11: OVERCOMING OUR OBSTACLES TO GRIEVING

p. 92   "This Land Is Your Land": The actual censored verse of Woodie Guthrie's song is "There was a big high wall there, that tried to stop me. The sign was painted, said 'Private Property.' But on the back side it didn't say nothing. This land was made for you and me," according to NPR's "The Story of Woodie Guthrie's 'This Land Is Your Land,'" from *All Things Considered*, February 15, 2012, www.npr .org/2000/07/03/1076186/this-land-is-your-land.

p. 96   "Believe me, if I could, I would": Anne Lamott, *Help, Thanks, Wow: The Three Essential Prayers* (New York: Riverhead Books, 2012), 17.

Chapter 12: Revealing Our Perspectives

p. 102   "Trust in the slow work of God": From Pierre Teilhard de Chardin, "Patient Trust," in *Hearts on Fire: Praying with Jesuits*, ed. Michael Harter (Chicago: Loyola Press, 1993), 102. The poem goes on to encourage us to "accept the anxiety of feeling yourself in suspense and incomplete."

Chapter 13: Fear of Falling

p. 108   "You learn how to recover from falling": Richard Rohr, *Falling Upward: A Spirituality for the Two Halves of Life* (San Francisco: Jossey-Bass, 2011), 28.

p. 110   "There is no human pain": Henri Nouwen, *Walk with Jesus: Stations of the Cross* (Maryknoll, NY: Orbis, 2004), ix.

Chapter 14: Grieve as We Can, Not as We Can't

p. 116   "Pray as you can, not as you can't": Attributed to Dom Chapman, according to Thelma Hall in *Too Deep for Words: Rediscovering Lectio Divina* (New York: Paulist Press, 1988), 40.

Chapter 15: Listening to the Shepherd

p. 122   "stilled, tranquil, in child-like trust": From Thomas Kelly's beautiful book *A Testament of Devotion* (New York: Harper, 1941), 74.

Chapter 16: Discoveries in the Dark

p. 130   *The Cloud of Unknowing*: Anonymous, *The Cloud of Unknowing* (New York: Doubleday, 1973) is a beautiful ex-

ploration of contemplative prayer written in the four-
teenth century.

p. 130   "Oh, night that led me": "The Dark Night of the Soul" is a
poem written by St John of the Cross, the sixteenth-
century Spanish mystic and saint (New York: Barnes &
Noble, 2005), 17.

p. 131   "learning to walk in the dark: Barbara Brown Taylor's book
Learning to Walk in the Dark (New York: HarperOne,
2014) explores the redeeming value of darkness.

p. 131   "Accept life": Sue Monk Kidd encourages us to "accept the
dark" in *When the Heart Waits: Spiritual Direction for
Life's Sacred Questions* (San Francisco: HarperCollins,
1990), 171.

CHAPTER 17: LETTING THE LIGHT IN THROUGH NATURE AND BEAUTY

p. 137   "There is a crack in everything God has made": Ralph
Waldo Emerson writes about cracks in *Compensation: An
Essay* (Boston: Houghton Mifflin, 1903), 30, and Leonard
Cohen adds to it in his song "Anthem" on the album *The
Future*, prod. Leonard Cohen (Columbia, 1992).

p. 138   "grace rarely comes": Belden Lane talks about grace in the
grotesque in *The Solace of Fierce Landscapes: Exploring
Desert and Mountain Spirituality* (New York: Oxford University Press, 1998), 32.

CHAPTER 22: GETTING UP AGAIN

p. 167   "holding his arm or inching along his side": The practice of
shiva is explained by Lauren Winner in *Mudhouse Sabbath*
(Brewster, MA: Paraclete, 2003), 35.

CHAPTER 23: LETTING GO

p. 170   "giving up the hope of a different or better yesterday":
This comes from *The Grief Recovery Handbook: The
Action Program for Moving Beyond Death, Divorce, and
Other Losses, Including Health, Career, and Faith* by John
W. James and Russell Friedman, 20th anniversary ed.

(New York: HarperCollins, 2009), 138. This is a great, pragmatic resource, as one might gather from its twenty-word title.

p. 171   "day by day remind yourself": St. Benedict's sobering reminder of death comes from *The Rule of St. Benedict,* chap. 4, "The Tools for Good Works." I used Joan Chittister's devotional version, *The Rule of Benedict: A Spirituality for the 21st Century* (New York: Crossroad, 1992), 61.

p. 173   twins arguing with each other: Henri Nouwen, *Our Greatest Gift: A Meditation on Dying and Caring* (New York: HarperCollins, 1994), 19-21.

p. 174   Prayer Practice: The Parting: This comes from Anthony De Mello's book *Wellsprings: A Book of Spiritual Exercises* (New York: Doubleday, 1985), 160-61.

Chapter 24: Traveling Companions

p. 181   "know all the words but none of the music": Sue Monk Kidd talks about coming to this place in life in *When the Heart Waits: Spiritual Direction for Life's Sacred Questions* (San Francisco: HarperCollins, 1990), 10.

p. 181   that "thing with feathers": Emily Dickinson's poem "Hope" can be found in *The Complete Poems of Emily Dickinson* (Boston: Back Bay Books, 1960), 116.

Chapter 25: Learning to Float

p. 185   "It is better to give than receive": Attributed to Vincent de Paul, in Ronald Rolheiser's book *Sacred Fire: A Vision for a Deeper Human and Christian Maturity* (New York: Image, 2014), 77.

p. 185   "If a thing is worth doing, it is worth doing badly": This is a line I quote way too much from the brilliant G. K. Chesterton, *What's Wrong with the World* ([US]: Feather Trail Press, 2009), 76.

p. 189   "Self-care is never a selfish act": From Parker Palmer, *Let Your Life Speak: Listening for the Voice of Vocation* (San Francisco: Jossey-Bass, 2000), 30-31.

p. 190   "Don't fight it": Frederick Buechner, *The Wizard's Tide*
              (San Francisco: Harper & Row, 1990), 62. Also titled *The*
              Christmas Tide.

p. 191   "Lie back, daughter": This is from a poem about a father
              teaching his daughter to float by Philip Booth, "First
              Lessons," in *Lifelines: Selected Poems 1950–1999* (New
              York: Penguin, 1999), 4.

p. 191   "And the end of all our exploring": T. S. Eliot's beautiful
              words are from his poem "Little Gidding," found in *Four*
              Quartets (New York: Mariner Books, 1968), 49.

Chapter 26: Coming Home to Our Broken Hallelujahs

p. 198   "a kiss of Jesus": Mother Teresa's understanding of suf-
              fering as being "a kiss of Jesus" can be found in *Words to*
              Love By (Notre Dame, IN: Ave Maria Press, 1983), 63-70.

p. 199   the U-bend article: "Age and Happiness: The U-bend of
              Life," *The Economist*, December 18, 2010, 33-36.

p. 199   "Grace . . . bats last": Anne Lamott, *Small Victories:*
              Spotting Improbable Moments of Grace (New York: River-
              head Books, 2014), 6.

p. 199   "Eden is the heart of Christ": Thomas Merton, *Dialogues*
              with Silence: Prayers and Drawings (San Francisco: Harper-
              SanFrancisco, 2001), 65.

About the Author

Beth Slevcove is a spiritual director, writer, mother and retreat leader who loves good books, good waves, good playgrounds and traveling old highways in an old VW camper van with her family.

She holds advanced degrees in education from Claremont Graduate University and theology from Fuller Theological Seminary. After completing training in spiritual direction at Fuller, Beth served Youth Specialties, a national youth ministry organization, as a spiritual director and co-led a spiritual direction and formation training program through Christian Formation and Direction Ministries. Beth currently co-leads the San Diego Spiritual Directors Association.

She lives with her husband, Joe, two kids, Allena and Akian, and dozens of Tijuana Surf Monkeys all named Chango from a surf company she runs.

Beth is passionate about helping people connect with the One who is already present, holding and healing us through all that life brings.

She can be reached at BethSlevSD@gmail.com.

IVP *Crescendo*
COURAGE. CONFIDENCE. CALLING.

Some voices challenge us. Others support or encourage us. Voices can move us to change our minds, draw close to God, discover a new spiritual gift. The voices of others are shaping who we are.

The voices behind IVP Crescendo join together to draw us into God's story. We'll discover God's work around the globe even as we learn to love the people around the corner. We'll have opportunity to heal our places of pain. We'll discover new ways to love our families. We'll hear God's voice speaking into our lives as we discover new places of influence.

IVP Crescendo invites you to join in the rising chorus

- *to listen to the voices of others*
- *to hear the voice of God*
- *and to grow your own voice in*

COURAGE. CONFIDENCE. CALLING.

ivpress.com/crescendo
ivpress.com/crescendo-social